Grades 1 & 2

An Unofficial Activity Book

The Super Fun Colossal Workbook for MINECRAFTERS

Sky Pony Press
New York

Copyright © 2021 by Hollan Publishing, Inc.
Minecraft® is a registered trademark of Notch Development AB.

The Minecraft game is copyright © Mojang AB.

Sky Pony Press books may be purchased in bulk at special discounts for sales promotion, corporate gifts, fund-raising, or educational purposes. Special editions can also be created to specifications. For details, contact the Special Sales Department, Sky Pony Press, 307 West 36th Street, 11th Floor, New York, NY 10018 or info@skyhorsepublishing.com.

Sky Pony® is a registered trademark of Skyhorse Publishing, Inc.®, a Delaware corporation.

Minecraft® is a registered trademark of Notch Development AB. The Minecraft game is copyright © Mojang AB.

Visit our website at www.skyponypress.com.

10 9 8 7 6 5 4 3 2 1

Library of Congress Cataloging-in-Publication Data is available on file.

Print ISBN: 978-1-5107-6302-9

Cover design by Kai Texel
Interior design by Noora Cox
Cover and interior illustrations by Amanda Brack

Printed in China

A NOTE TO PARENTS

Welcome to a super world of colossal fun and learning with a Minecrafting twist. When you want to reinforce classroom skills, break up screen time, or enhance kids' problem-solving skills at home, it's crucial to have high-interest, kid-friendly learning materials.

The Super Fun Colossal Workbook for Minecrafters transforms educational lessons into exciting adventures complete with diamond swords, zombies, skeletons, and creepers. With colorful illustrations and familiar characters to guide them through, your kids will feel like winners from start to finish. The best part: The educational content in this workbook is aligned with National Common Core Standards for 1st and 2nd grade. So everything in this book matches up with what your children are learning and will be learning—to build confidence and keep them ahead of the curve.

Whether it's the joy of seeing their favorite game come to life on each page or the thrill of solving challenging problems just like Steve and Alex, there is something in *The Super Fun Colossal Workbook for Minecrafters* to engage every kind of learner. Happy adventuring!

CONTENTS

* *While all of these projects are kid-friendly and encourage little ones to get involved, some of the experiments require or strongly benefit from parental supervision. These are marked with redstone dust.*

SOCIAL SKILLS FOR MINECRAFTERS

ME AS A PLAYER

Create a player who looks like you. Add hair, eyes, nose, mouth, clothes, and other details. Finish the sentences below.

My hair is ....

My eyes are ....

My skin is ....

My shirt is ....

My pants are ....

WHO AM I?

People and mobs have characteristics. Characteristics are ways to describe a person or thing. Read these characteristics to identify each mob. Draw a picture of each mob.

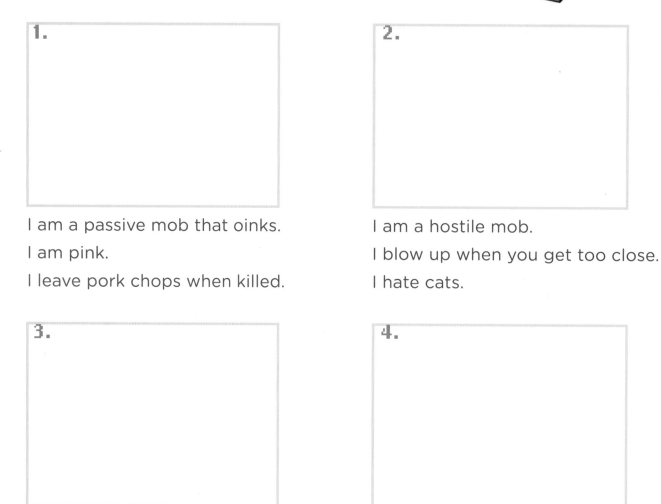

1.

I am a passive mob that oinks.

I am pink.

I leave pork chops when killed.

2.

I am a hostile mob.

I blow up when you get too close.

I hate cats.

3.

I am a mob you can tame and ride.

I come in many colors.

I am not a donkey or a mule.

4.

I have eight legs.

I climb walls.

I drop string when killed.

WHO AM I?

Make up your own Who Am I? cards describing people or characters you know and see if your friends and family can guess correctly.

MY BIOME

Draw your biome where you live.

THE SKIN YOU'RE IN

In Minecraft, you can try on different "skins" or make your character look different ways. In real life, we need to learn to love the skin we're in.

Draw a picture of yourself below. Put a star next to any physical features you love, such as your freckles.

TURN IT AROUND

Have features you don't love? Most people do! But nothing is all bad.

Name one thing you don't love, and then turn it upside down: come up with a reason why that feature can be good. We'll get you started.

I'm too green!

But that makes you super sneaky. You blend in with trees and bushes!

A feature you don't love: _____

Why it can be a good thing: _____

_____

_____

Need help? **Ask an adult. Was there a feature they didn't like as a kid that they're actually proud of now?**

THE ONE AND ONLY YOU

Imagine a world where everyone looks and acts exactly the same. How boring would that be? Our differences make us interesting!

Circle the two villagers below who look exactly the same.

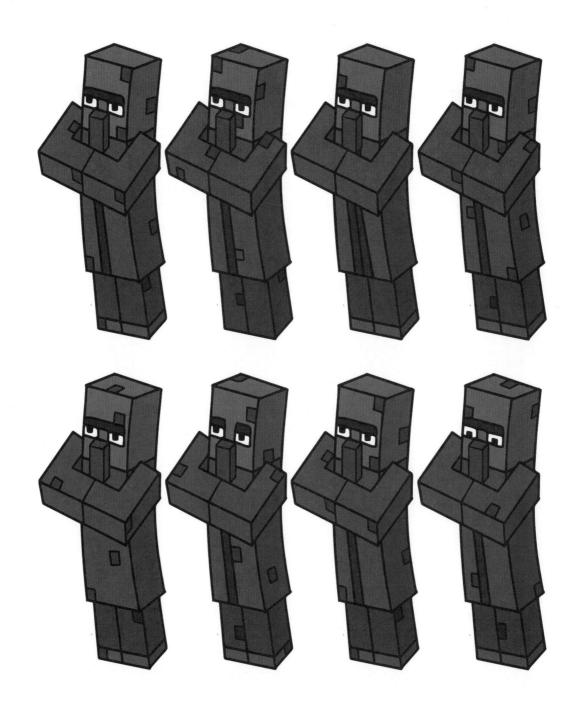

That was tough, right? In the real world, no two people are exactly alike.

What makes you unique? How are you different from anyone else you know? List three ways:

1. _____

_____

_____

2. _____

_____

_____

3. _____

_____

_____

Hint: If you need help, ask a friend or family member what they think is most special about you.

THIS OR THAT?

Ocelots love salmon and wolves love bones. Everyone has likes and dislikes—they make us unique.

*Circle the word in each pair that YOU like best, and then share the quiz with a friend. Did you choose different things? Good! Talk about why, and remember: it's **okay** to disagree.*

ocelot	OR	wolf
diamonds	OR	emeralds
bow and arrow	OR	sword
minecart	OR	Elytra wings
mooshroom	OR	llama
potion of Invisibility	OR	potion of Water Breathing
Desert Biome	OR	Cold Taiga Biome
iron golem	OR	snow golem
riding a horse	OR	riding a pig
red mushroom	OR	brown mushroom

JUST THE WAY I LIKE IT

Draw what you like and dislike in Minecraft.
Your likes and dislikes make you unique.

Mob	Biome
I like _____ .	I like _____ .
I dislike _____ .	I dislike _____ .
Food	Activity
I like _____ .	I like _____ .
I dislike _____ .	I dislike _____ .

THE THINGS YOU CAN DO

Confidence comes from knowing your strengths, or what you do well. Maybe you're a good listener or team player. Maybe you're great at soccer or playing piano. Everyone has different strengths, even in Minecraft.

Check off the Minecraft activities that you do well:

- [ ] Mine for blocks
- [ ] Build houses
- [ ] Craft with a crafting table
- [ ] Grow crops
- [ ] Care for animals
- [ ] Tame wolves
- [ ] Build minecart tracks
- [ ] Brew potions
- [ ] Navigate with maps
- [ ] Battle mobs
- [ ] Enchant items
- [ ] Invent with redstone
- [ ] Work together with friends!

ARMED WITH CONFIDENCE

Feeling confident is like wearing enchanted armor. When you know what you like and what you can do, you feel stronger and happier.

Decorate this chest plate with pictures that represent you— your activities, hobbies, and favorite things.

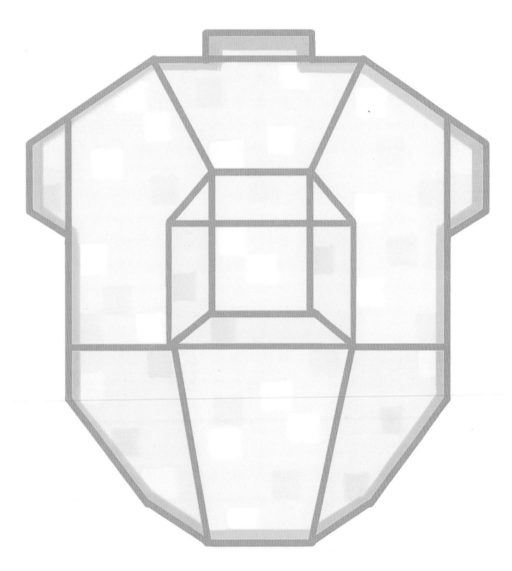

HOW'S STEVE FEELING?

Draw a line to match Steve's emotions.

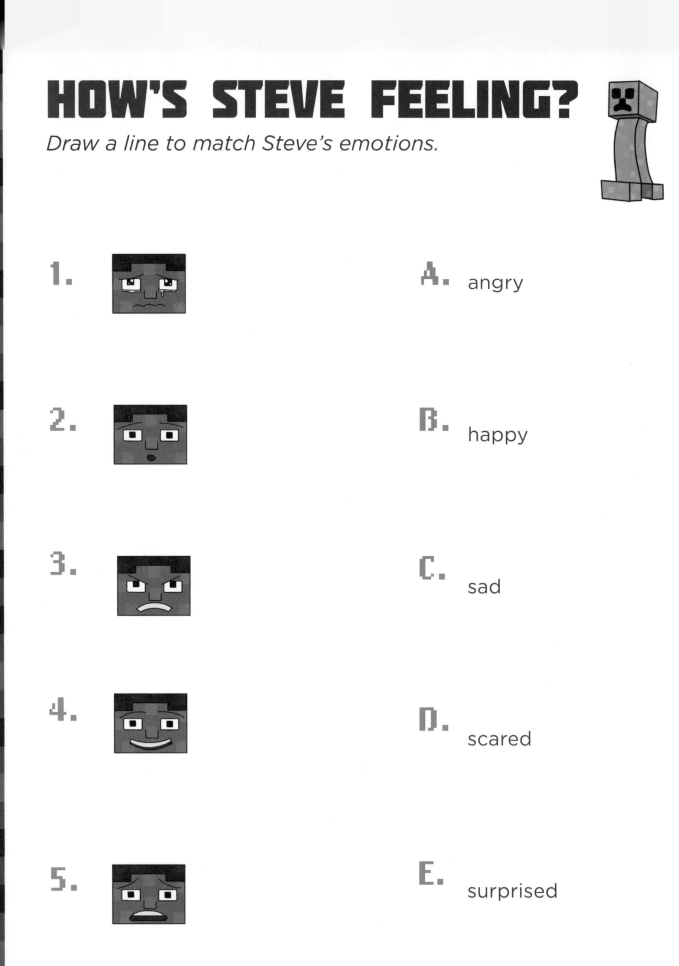

1.

2.

3.

4.

5.

A. angry

B. happy

C. sad

D. scared

E. surprised

EMOTIONS

Write the emotion that describes how each mob is feeling.

| sad | embarrassed | proud |
| bored | angry | happy |

1. Horse is _____.
He tripped and fell in front of everyone.

2. Witch is _____.
She has no friends.

3. Alex is _____.
She loves being with pig.

4. Steve is _____.
He made a wonderful sword.

5. Creepers are _____.
They lose their temper often!

6. Ghast is _____.
She has nothing to do.

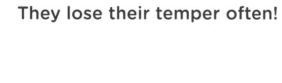

BAD MOOD BUSTERS

You can't dance your heart out and still be in a bad mood—it's almost impossible! There are lots of ways to boost your mood.

Circle three things that you'll try the next time you're feeling down:

❅ Go outside

❅ Make up a dance

❅ Play with a pet

❅ Talk to a friend or family member

❅ Watch a funny video or show

❅ Play video games with a friend

❅ Take three deep breaths

❅ Write in a journal

❅ Memorize song lyrics

❅ Draw a doodle

BE-FRIEND YOURSELF

If your confidence starts to slip, give yourself a pep talk—just like you would with a friend. If you practice speaking kindly to yourself, you'll have the words to use whenever you need a boost.

Fill in the blanks below.

[Your name here] _____,

I really like how you _____,

_____, and _____.

You're already good at _____. And you've

been practicing _____, so I know

you're going to get better and better.

[Your name here] _____, you rock!

WEBS OF WORRY

Worries are like cobwebs that keep you from moving forward. Are you worried about making mistakes? Not reaching your goal? Embarrassing yourself?

Write the word "So" in front of each of the worries below.

_____ what if I make a mistake?

At least you tried. You probably learned something too, which means you're one step closer to reaching your goal. So get up and keep going!

_____ what if I embarrass myself in front of everyone?

People aren't watching that closely. They have worries of their own. And if they DO see you do something embarrassing? Laugh with them and move on. They'll move on soon too.

_____ what if someone else can do it better?

Reaching your goal isn't about beating anyone else. It's about doing what YOU said you were going to do. The only way you can "lose" is not to try at all.

You just pulled out your "so what?" shears and snipped your worries down to size. Feel better?

POWER TO IMAGINE

Ignoring teasing and bullying is harder than it sounds! Tap into your imagination to make it easier.

Circle one answer for each statement below, and then picture it in your mind. The more you practice mind tricks, the easier it is to use them when you need them!

✳ Pretend the bully is a pesky parrot or a clucking chicken.

✳ Pretend you just splashed the bully with a potion of Invisibility or Slowness.

 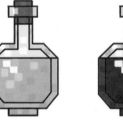 

✳ Imagine you are soaring high above the bully with Elytra wings or on the back of the Ender Dragon.

STANDING UP TO BULLIES

People who bully are trying to take away your power—and confidence.

How do you stop them? Memorize the motto hidden in the secret message below. To decode the message, circle each word that comes right after the word GHAST.

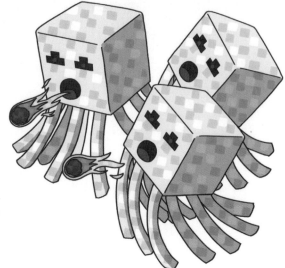

GHAST NOBODY BATTLES GHAST CAN FLY WITH GHAST TAKE GHAST AWAY FROM THE NETHER GHAST MY IRON SWORD GHAST POWER FIREBALLS

Write the words you circled here:

_____

_____

Remember this motto the next time you need to stand strong.

A BULLY-PROOF BODY

How confident are you? Your body gives off clues. Kids without confidence might slouch or slump their shoulders. They might hang their head or stare at the ground. But confident kids look like *this*:

Look in the mirror and practice a confident pose. Imagine yourself in enchanted armor, as if nothing anyone says or does can harm you. Can you check off each box?

☐ Head high

☐ Shoulders back

☐ Standing tall

☐ Eyes up or straight ahead

When you practice looking confident on the outside, you start *feeling* more confident on the inside. And that'll help you stand up to bullying.

KINDESS MAP

Think of people you know at school, in your neighborhood or community, and even at home. Who could use some kindness?

Write at least one name in each area on the map below. How many names can you come up with?

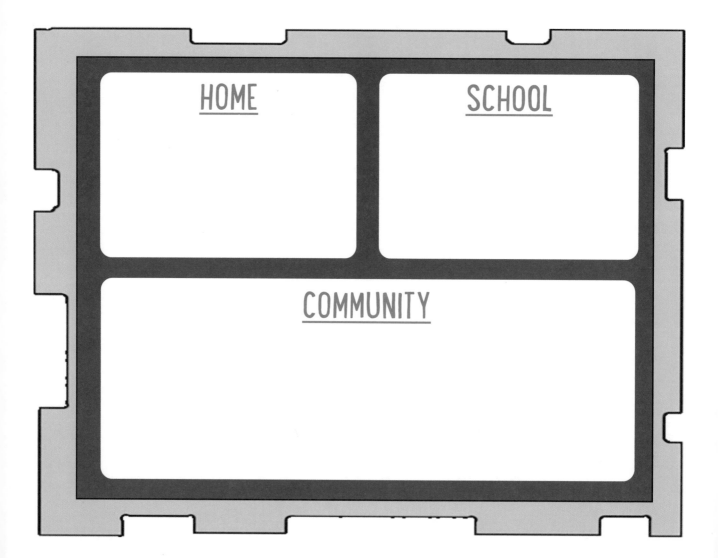

HOME

SCHOOL

COMMUNITY

SPLASH POTIONS OF CONFIDENCE

You use splash potions to heal yourself and others in Minecraft. Imagine that you could do the same thing in real life!

For each potion bottle below, write someone's name and one kind thing you could do to boost their confidence.

NAME:

NAME:

NAME:

What I can do:

What I can do:

What I can do:

_____ _____ _____

_____ _____ _____

_____ _____ _____

_____ _____ _____

Now, armed with your splash potions, can you go out and spread kindness and confidence?

FAMILIES

Families are made of people. Every family is different. Describe your family. Use the word box if you need help.

Even zombie villagers have families.

mom	stepmom	dad	stepdad
brother	sister		grandma
grandpa	aunt	uncle	cousins

1. I live with _____

_____ .

2. I have _____ brothers and _____ sisters.

3. Sometimes I visit _____

_____

_____ .

4. I have _____ aunts and _____ uncles.

5. I have _____ cousins.

MY FAMILY

Draw a picture of your family. Label the picture with the names of the people in your family.

Hanging with our family is a blast.

FRIENDS

Look at what friends do. Then write about what you and your friends like to do.

Friends have fun together.

Friends are kind to each other.

Friends spend time together.

Friends laugh together.

_____

_____

_____

_____

_____

_____

FRIENDS

Check each box that tells something a good friend would do.

We all need a friend.

☐ **1.** take turns

☐ **2.** share

☐ **3.** push in line

☐ **4.** say something nice

☐ **5.** not let someone play with you

☐ **6.** act rudely

☐ **7.** give a high five

☐ **8.** listen

☐ **9.** tattle

☐ **10.** lie

BLOCK BREATHING

Feeling a little stressed? Try this breathing exercise.

Sit or lie in a comfortable position.

1. Take a deep breath in through your nose as you slowly count 1, 2, 3, 4.

2. Hold your breath for the count of four.

3. Exhale through your mouth slowly for the count of four.

4. Pause for the count of four before inhaling.

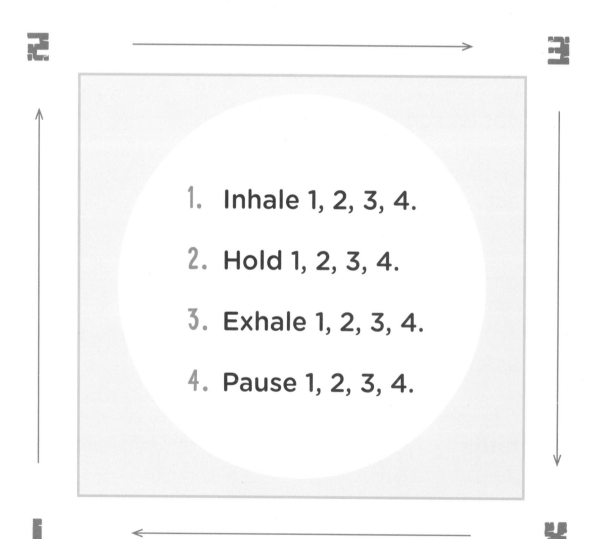

1. Inhale 1, 2, 3, 4.

2. Hold 1, 2, 3, 4.

3. Exhale 1, 2, 3, 4.

4. Pause 1, 2, 3, 4.

BREATHE LIKE ME

Practice breathing slowly like each animal.

Inhale slowly through your mouth.

Breathe like a snake.

Sssss . . .

Breathe like a bee.

Hmmmm . . .

Breathe like an ocelot.

Aaahh . . .

Breathe like a dragon.

Hhooo . . .

Then exhale slowly, making the sound each mob makes.

THE POWER OF YET

*When you get discouraged, remember the power of **yet**. Help Steve get some confidence by adding the word **yet** to each sentence.*

1. I can't do this _____ .

2. I don't understand this _____ .

3. This doesn't make sense to me _____ .

4. This doesn't work _____ .

5. I'm not good at this _____ .

*Now list some things that you can't do **yet**.*

_____

_____

_____

_____

_____

_____

GROWTH MINDSET THOUGHTS

A growth mindset is a way of thinking that helps you grow and learn. Draw a line from Steve's sad thoughts to thoughts that help Steve grow.

SAD STEVE

HAPPY STEVE

1. Oops, I made a mistake.

2. I'll never learn this.

3. I give up.

4. This is boring.

5. I'm afraid to try.

6. This is too hard.

A. I will try something new.

B. I never give up.

C. Mistakes help me grow.

D. Who can I ask for help?

E. I can learn to do this.

F. I can do it!

Write your favorite growth mindset thought.

_____

ATTITUDE OF GRATITUDE

Having an attitude of gratitude helps you improve your mood! Write one thing you are grateful for that begins with each letter of the alphabet.

A _____

B _____

C _____

D _____

E _____

F _____

G _____

H _____

I _____

J _____

K _____

L _____

M _____

N _____

O _____

P _____

Q _____

R _____

S _____

T _____

U _____

V _____

W _____

X _____

Y _____

Z _____

GUARDIAN HAS GRIT

*Grit is what makes you strong enough to reach your goals. Guardian has grit . . . how about you? Write about how you show grit by **g**rowing, being **r**eady, being **i**nterested, and being **t**ough.*

GROWING

I grow when I _____

_____ .

READY

I show I am ready by _____

_____ .

INTERESTED

I am interested in _____

_____ .

TOUGH

I prove I am tough when _____

_____ .

KEEP CALM

Help Creeper calm down. Write about a situation that upset Creeper. Then share a way to help Creeper calm down.

CHILL OUT

ACCEPT YOUR FEELINGS

LISTEN TO YOUR THOUGHTS

MIND YOUR BEHAVIOR

Creeper got really upset when _____

_____ .

To help himself chill out, Creeper _____

_____ .

Creeper listened to his thoughts. He was thinking _____

_____ .

But Creeper chose to mind his behavior. He decided it was

best to _____

_____ .

GOLEM'S GOAL

Follow the maze to help Iron Golem reach his goal to collect poppies.

START

FINISH

WITHER'S WISDOM

To decode Wither's goal-setting wisdom, circle only the words that immediately follow the word GOAL.

GOAL   IF   SOMETIMES   TRY   GOAL   YOU
NEVER   ALWAYS   GOAL   CAN   GO   KEEP   GOAL
DREAM   SOMETIMES   YOU   THE   GOAL   IT
THERE   ARE   YOU   GOAL   YOU   ROCK   SO   GOAL
CAN   TRY   NO   GOAL   DO   TRY   BEST   GOAL   IT

Write Wither's wisdom here:

_____

_____

Write your goal here:

_____

MINECRAFT GOALS

Unscramble the words to discover some goals set by mobs and players in Minecraft.

1. The main goal in Survival mode is to **V I R V U S E**.

_____

2. Another goal in Survival mode is to build a **S H O E U**.

_____

3. In Creative mode a goal is to craft **L O S T O**.

_____

4. Snow Golem's goal is to avoid **S C R R E E E P**.

_____

5. Iron Golem's goal is to protect **G R A I L V E L S**.

_____

MY GOAL

Some goals take practice to reach. Write a goal you have.
Then write some steps you will take to reach your goal.
Practice your goal. Draw a picture of you reaching your goal.

My goal: _____

Steps to reach my goal:

_____

_____

_____

Time to practice!

Color a heart each time you practice.

Here is me reaching my goal:

CONFIDENCE CROSSWORD

Complete the puzzle.

WORD LIST

BREATH

CALM

CONFIDENCE

GRIT

GROWTH

HOME

KIND

ONE

SET A GOAL

YET

ACROSS

3 A belief in yourself

5 Remember the power of _____ when you want to give up.

7 A place where you live

9 Strength to reach your goals

10 Do this to grow. (3 words)

DOWN

1 Friends are _____ to one another.

2 To calm yourself, take a deep _____.

4 A quiet peaceful feeling

6 A _____ mindset helps you reach your goals.

8 You are _____ of a kind.

STEM QUEST CHALLENGES

You may have used **BAKING SODA** and **VINEGAR** to make "lava" bubble out of a model volcano, but now you can use those same ingredients to create an **EXPLOSION**. Here, you will have to act quickly and get out of the way before your TNT bag's chemical reactions make a big mess of things. This is the perfect outdoor **STEM** project for curious Minecrafters.

INSTRUCTIONS

1. Write "TNT" on the zipper-seal bag with a permanent marker.
2. Line a table with wax paper. Open a facial tissue (if it is two-ply, only use one layer) and lay it flat on the wax paper. In the center, place 3 tablespoons of baking soda. Add 10–12 drops of yellow food coloring to the baking soda. Carefully fold the tissue around the baking soda to make a packet. Set the baking soda packet aside.
3. Carefully pour the vinegar into the zipper-seal bag.
4. Add 4–6 drops of red food coloring to the vinegar.
5. Add a generous squirt of dish soap to the vinegar.
6. Take your project outside.
7. Zip the bag partway closed.
8. Place the tissue paper with the baking soda in the bag of vinegar.
9. Quickly zip the bag completely closed.
10. Move away from the bag and observe.

MATERIALS

- black permanent marker
- zipper-seal freezer bag (quart)
- 1 tissue
- wax paper
- 3 tbsp baking soda
- 1 cup vinegar
- dish soap
- 10–12 drops yellow food coloring
- 4–6 drops red food coloring

WHAT REALLY HAPPENED?

❄ Hopefully, your TNT bag bubbled, expanded, and then popped. Pretty cool! Inside the bag, the baking soda and vinegar mixed to create an acid-base reaction. In the process, the two chemicals created the gas carbon dioxide.

❄ Gas needs room to expand, so carbon dioxide filled the bag until the bag could not hold any more gas. As a result, the bag popped.

YOUR TURN TO EXPERIMENT

Think of ways you could change the experiment. What would happen if you changed the size of the bag, the temperature of the vinegar, or the amount of baking soda? **MAKE ONE OF THESE CHANGES AND RECORD YOUR OBSERVATIONS BELOW.**

OBSERVATIONS:

FREE-FLOATING GHAST

Use static to make an object move.

Don't be shocked by this hair-raising experiment! **STATIC ELECTRICITY** makes objects stick together by creating **OPPOSITE CHARGES**. In this activity, you'll make a tissue-paper ghast that can float. All you have to do is use a balloon to harness the power of static electricity.

INSTRUCTIONS

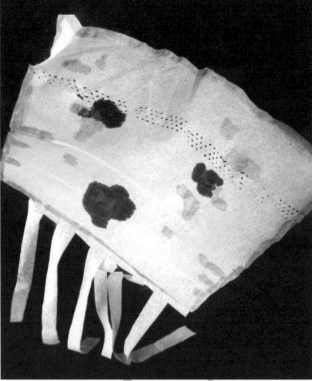

1. Cut a ghast shape out of the tissue. Feel free to add details like eyes, a mouth, and long legs.

2. If you are using tissues, carefully pull the two layers of tissue apart so that you just have one layer—now you have 2 ghasts!

3. Blow up the balloon and tie the end.

4. Rub the balloon very quickly through your hair for at least 10 seconds. (Or you can rub the balloon on a piece of wool fabric.) This adds static charge.

5. Slowly bring the charged balloon near the ghast. The ghast will start to rise up toward the balloon, and it might even try to attach itself to the balloon.

6. Practice with the balloon and the ghast. You might get good enough to have the ghast float over the surface of the table.

MATERIALS

- tissue or tissue paper
- scissors
- balloon
- your head (or a piece of wool fabric)

WHAT REALLY HAPPENED?

✳ Rubbing a balloon on your head created static electricity. Static electricity is the buildup of electrical charge in an object. Static electricity causes objects to stick together, like when a sock sticks to a fuzzy sweater in the laundry. This happens when objects have opposite charges (positive and negative) that attract.

✳ When you rubbed the balloon on your head, you created a charge on the balloon. When you brought the charged balloon close to the lightweight tissue, the tissue was attracted to the balloon. This caused the tissue to move toward the balloon.

YOUR TURN TO EXPERIMENT

Make floating ghasts out of different types of paper—facial tissues, bathroom tissues, tissue paper, or white paper are options to consider. **WHICH TYPE OF PAPER WAS EASIEST TO CONTROL?**

OBSERVATIONS:

I ♥ PIXELS

Use coordinates to draw like a computer.

When you open Minecraft on a computer, you can see all of your favorite characters on the screen. Whether it's a creeper, a zombie, or a witch, your computer needs **NUMBER INFORMATION** to know how to draw these mobs on the screen. In this activity, you will learn how computers use **COORDINATES** (numbers that give a location) to make those pictures.

INSTRUCTIONS

Coordinates are numbers on a grid that give a location. In the case of a computer graphics coordinate system, the first number tells the computer how many location steps across, and the second number tells the computer how many steps down.

For example, if you wanted to put a red dot in the middle of the graph on the right, you would give the computer these coordinates:

(3, 3 red)

The first number tells the computer to go 3 pixels to the right (starting at the upper left-hand corner of the screen).

The second number tells the computer to drop 3 squares down. The word red tells the computer to fill in that pixel with the color red.

0	1	2	3	4	5
1	→		↓		
2			↓		
3					
4					
5					

Now *you* be the computer. Use the coordinates below to draw a smiley face on the screen at right. The first pixel is drawn for you: 2 to the right, 2 down, black.

See if you can use the coordinates to draw the rest.

———————————

(2, 2 black) ■   (6, 4 black) ■   (3, 6 black) ■
(5, 2 black) ■   (2, 5 black) ■   (4, 6 black) ■
(1, 4 black) ■   (5, 5 black) ■

0	1	2	3	4	5	6
1						
2		■				
3						
4						
5						
6						

YOUR TURN TO EXPERIMENT

❋ Use graph paper to represent your computer screen (or use a white piece of paper to trace the grid shown above). Number the grid as shown and shade in the eyes and mouth of a creeper face.

❋ Write the coordinates for the pixels you colored in. Have a friend or family member be the computer and try to draw a creeper face on a new paper using only your coordinates. Did it work?

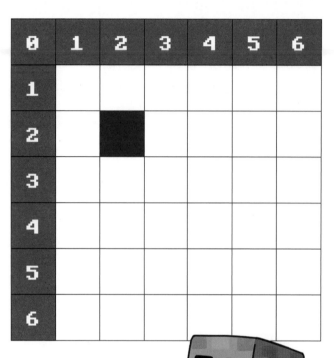

PIXEL POWER

Computers draw images using pixels, which are tiny points of color. Pixels make up the images you see on computer games like Minecraft. Minecraft uses thousands of images with very noticeable pixels.

EFFERVESCING POTION

Make a bubbling chemical reaction in a bottle.

Potions in Minecraft have lots of uses. They can help you in combat by giving you strength, healing, or swiftness. This potion isn't safe to drink, but it's a lot of fun to make and watch. You'll use Alka-Seltzer tablets to **CREATE BUBBLES OF CARBON DIOXIDE** that make the potion move and dance. If this were a potion, it would be called the potion of Knowledge.

INSTRUCTIONS

1. Measure 2 cups of vegetable oil and pour into your glass jar or bottle.

2. Add 1 cup of water. Record your observation in the table below.

3. Add 5–6 drops of food coloring.

4. Place your jar over a pie tin or cookie sheet.

5. Remove one Alka-Seltzer tablet from the wrapper and break into 4 pieces.

6. Add one piece of the Alka-Seltzer tablet at a time and enjoy the show! Record your observations in the table below.

7. You can continue adding Alka-Seltzer tablets to continue the reaction.

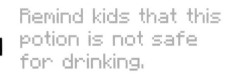 Remind kids that this potion is not safe for drinking.

WHAT REALLY HAPPENED?

❋ You may have heard the phrase "oil and water do not mix." This is why: when water is added to oil, it sinks to the bottom and the oil floats to the top. Oil floats because it is less dense (the molecules are packed more loosely) than the water.

❋ Adding Alka-Seltzer to oil and water started a chemical reaction. The Alka-Seltzer reacted with water to form carbon dioxide gas. The gas attached itself to a few water molecules, and together the water molecules and carbon dioxide made bubbles that floated to the surface. When it reached the surface of the "potion," the bubbles popped and released the carbon dioxide into the air. Then, the water molecules (now empty bubbles) returned to the bottom of the jar.

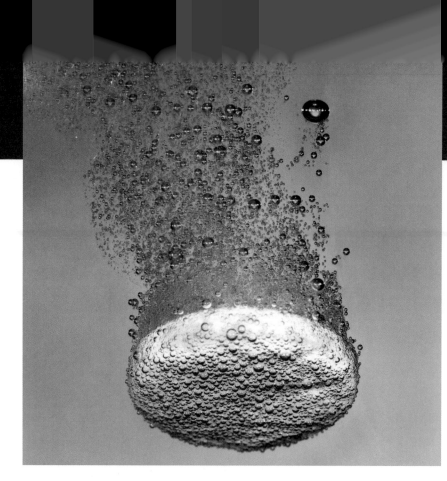

MATERIALS

- 2 cups vegetable oil
- glass jar or bottle (large enough to contain 3 cups of liquid, plus space for bubbling)
- 1 cup water
- 5–6 drops food coloring
- pie tin or cookie sheet for containing spills
- 1 box of Alka-Seltzer tablets

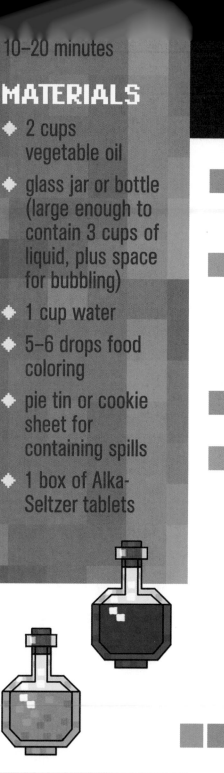

YOUR TURN TO EXPERIMENT

❋ Try adding a few drops of a different food coloring. What happens?

❋ Time the reaction from when you place the Alka-Seltzer tablet in the oil-water mixture to when the bubbles form and move. How long does it take? How long does it last?

❋ How could Steve or Alex use a bubbling potion like this one in the game of Minecraft? What effect would it have? Would it make a player fly? Would it make creepers stop exploding? **USE THE SPACE BELOW TO EXPLAIN.**

CRYSTALLINE DIAMONDS

Witness the process of nucleation.

Diamonds are an **IMPORTANT RESOURCE** in Minecraft. They can be used to make armor, weapons, and beacons. In the real world, **CRYSTALS** are used to make watches, tools, and even surgery scalpels! Learn how to make your own spectacular **CRYSTALLINE DIAMONDS** in this experiment that allows you to observe over time.

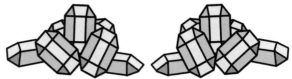

INSTRUCTIONS

1. Choose a chenille wire and food coloring to match the color of crystal you would like to make.

2. Twist 2–3 inches of the chenille wires into a shape (sphere, cube, teardrop).

3. Tie one end of the thread around the chenille wire.

4. Attach the chenille wire to the skewer using the thread. The shape needs to hang into the pot so that it is submerged but not touching the bottom of the pot. Set the skewer with the chenille wire hanging down into the empty pot. After you are satisfied with the length of the thread, remove the skewer and chenille wire and set aside.

5. Fill the pot with water and add the food coloring.

6. With the help of a grown-up, bring the colored water to a simmer and add Borax powder until the solution is supersaturated. You will know that you have a supersaturated solution when a little Borax remains at the bottom of the pot. At this point, you can turn off the stove.

7. Lay the skewer across the top of the pot with the chenille wire hanging down into the Borax solution.

8. Cover the pot with the lid, then use aluminum foil to seal in the heat. Layer towels over the top of the pot to keep the heat in the pot as long as possible.

9. Wait 24 hours until the pot has completely cooled before removing the crystal formation.

MATERIALS

- chenille wires
  (2–3 inches)
- thread
  (about 3–4 inches)
- skewer
- large pot with lid
- water
- food coloring
- Borax
- aluminum foil
- towels

WHAT REALLY HAPPENED?

※ Crystals start growing by a process called nucleation. The particles in the solution (Borax in this activity) are attracted to each other and form bonds. The particles naturally arrange in a regular and repeated pattern to form a solid called a crystal.

YOUR TURN TO EXPERIMENT

※ Make a variety of different crystals. Try growing different colors of crystals or use other substances, such as sugar, salt, alum, or Epsom salts to create them.

※ Consider waiting longer than 24 hours to pull your crystals out of the solution next time. What happens to the size of the crystal if you wait?

Note to parents: To return your crystal pot to normal, simply fill with water and return it to the stove on medium low. After everything has turned back to a liquid, you can pour the contents down the drain.

MINIATURE BOW-AND-ARROW

Watch physics in action.

Bow and arrows are handy weapons for defeating creepers and skeletons from a safe distance, but have you ever thought about how they work? This experiment lets you create your own working bow and arrow so you can see **ENERGY TRANSFER** and **TRAJECTORIES** in action.

INSTRUCTIONS

1. Have an adult use the glue gun to place a drop of hot glue in the opening of 1 wooden cube.

2. Push a dowel rod through the glue and into the hole until it is flush with the other side of the cube. This will be the front of your bow.

3. Repeat Step 1 with a second cube and add the new cube to the other end of the dowel rod.

4. Have an adult glue a stepped row of three additional cubes to one side of a cube attached to the dowel rod (see photo). Make sure the holes face the same direction as those of the first cube. Repeat this process on the other side of the dowel rod to create the frame of your bow.

5. Cut the rubber band.

6. After the glue has dried and hardened on the frame, insert one end of the rubber band through the last cube you attached. Then insert it through a bead.

7. Tie the end of the rubber band to keep it from sliding back through the bead.

8. Repeat Steps 6–7 for the other side of the bow.

9. Use the remaining dowel rods as arrows. Grip the dowel rod with one hand and pull the arrow back (pinching it against the rubber band). Release and let the arrow soar!

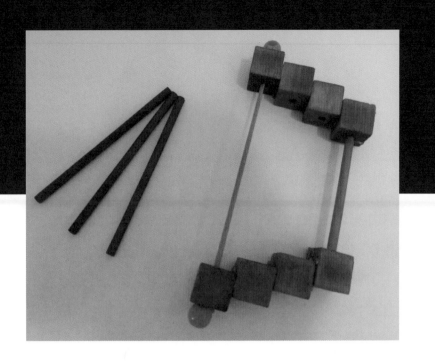

WHAT REALLY HAPPENED?

❋ When you pulled back on the bowstring, you used your muscles to exert a force on the string. When you let go, your energy was transferred to the rubber band, which used the energy to launch the arrow forward. The more you pull back on the bowstring, the more energy is transferred, which makes the arrow fly farther.

❋ When an arrow is released, it follows an arch-shaped path, called a trajectory. When you shoot it, the arrow is catapulted forward and upward. As it loses energy, gravity pulls the arrow back toward the Earth.

YOUR TURN TO EXPERIMENT

❋ Try changing the sizes of the bow and arrows. What size combination shoots the arrows the longest distance? What other household objects can you use as arrows? How about cotton-tipped swabs?

TIME

15–20 minutes

MATERIALS

◆ glue gun and hot glue sticks

◆ 8 miniature wooden cubes with center holes (available at most craft stores with dowel rods included)

◆ 2–4 small dowel rods

◆ rubber band

◆ 2 small beads

NEWTON'S FLYING BAT

Create a bat that flies using Newton's Third Law of Motion.

Explore a cave in Minecraft and, chances are, you'll see some bats hanging upside down or you'll hear them shrieking as they fly overhead. While creepy, these passive mobs won't hurt you. In this activity, they'll actually teach you a little about **PHYSICS**. Have fun making a Minecraft balloon bat that flies according to **NEWTON'S THIRD LAW OF MOTION**: For every action, there is an equal and opposite reaction.

INSTRUCTIONS

1. Using a marker, color the straw black. Allow it to dry. This is the bat's back.

2. Attach crepe paper "wings" to the center of the straw with glue dots.

3. Fold a piece of crepe paper into a rectangle to use as the bat's head. Glue small crepe paper ears and googly eyes to it to create the head.

4. Attach the head to the straw with glue dots.

5. Thread the fishing line (or dental floss) through the straw.

6. Tie the tail end of the fishing line onto a chair or other piece of furniture. Tie the other end, extending from the bat's head, to another higher piece of furniture.

7. Place two glue dots on the bat's belly area, near the center of the length of straw.

8. Inflate the balloon and pinch (do not tie) the end with your fingers or a clothespin to keep it inflated.

9. Attach the balloon to the glue dots on the bat's belly so the pinched end is pointing back behind the bat.

10. When you are ready, let go and watch your bat fly!

TIME
30 minutes prep plus drying time

MATERIALS
- black permanent marker
- plastic straw
- black crepe paper
- glue dots
- scissors
- googly eyes
- 4–6 feet of fishing line or unwaxed dental floss
- 1 black balloon
- electrician's tape or black duct tape
- clothespin (optional)

WHAT REALLY HAPPENED?

❋ **ISAAC NEWTON** was a famous scientist. He was the first person to explain why objects drop when they are released in the air. He called the force that causes this gravity. He studied motion and wrote three very important laws or rules about it. This activity demonstrated Newton's Third Law of Motion, which explains that for every action, there is an equal and opposite reaction. When air traveled out of the balloon in one direction, it caused the balloon to move in the opposite direction.

YOUR TURN TO EXPERIMENT

❋ Have a bat-flying contest with a friend. Set up multiple zip lines for the bats and race to see whose bat is the fastest.

❋ Does the size of the balloon influence the distance that the bat travels? Try using larger and smaller balloons.

NETHER LAVA

Make bubbling lava to understand density and see how solids dissolve.

Turn your kitchen into the **NETHER** when you create jars of **OIL-AND-WATER LAVA** that bubbles just like the lava in your favorite game. Is it hot? No, but it's as close to real lava as you'll want to get, and it lets you watch what happens when a solid travels through liquids of **DIFFERENT DENSITIES.**

INSTRUCTIONS

1. Fill a clear jar or glass three-quarters full of water.

2. Add 5–10 drops of red food coloring.

3. Slowly pour the vegetable oil on top of the water.

4. Sprinkle some salt on top of the oil.

5. Carefully observe the lava float up and down in the water.

6. You can continue adding salt and keep watching.

WHAT REALLY HAPPENED?

❊ Oil floats because it is less dense than water.

❊ The salt is denser than the oil, so it sinks. When it passes through the layer of oil, some of the oil gets stuck to the salt. When the salt and oil reach the water, the salt dissolves in the water, and the oil floats back up to the surface.

MATERIALS

- clear jar or glass
- water
- red food coloring
- ¼ cup of vegetable oil
- salt (1 or more teaspoons)

YOUR TURN TO EXPERIMENT

Swap out the salt for other solid ingredients that dissolve easily, such as sugar or baking soda. What happens?

How long can you keep the reaction going by adding more salt? Chart your longest times here:

Amount of Salt	Reaction Time (in seconds)

SQUID CHROMATOGRAPHY
Find hidden colors in squid ink.

If you play Minecraft, you know that **SQUID** are passive mobs that drop ink sacs you can later use to create dyes. They use their tentacles to swim about, and they **RELEASE A CLOUD OF BLACK INK** to hide their escape when a player attacks. Real-life squid shoot black ink, too. If you could examine the ink more closely, you might find something surprisingly colorful. In this experiment, you'll use **CHROMATOGRAPHY** to see the **HIDDEN COLORS** that make up black ink.

INSTRUCTIONS

1. Cover your work surface with newspaper.

2. Using the marker, draw a black circle (a little bigger than the size of a quarter) in the center of the coffee filter and color it in darkly.

3. Place a cotton ball on top of the black circle.

4. Use the eyedropper to saturate the cotton ball with rubbing alcohol.

5. Secure the coffee filter around the cotton ball with the rubber band.

6. Cut into the coffee filter from the edges to give the squid eight legs.

7. Prop the squid up on its legs and watch! If nothing seems to be happening, you can add more rubbing alcohol to the top of the squid with the eyedropper.

8. Allow the ink to separate into various colors (the colors will differ depending upon the marker that is used) over the next 30–60 minutes.

TIME

30 minutes

MATERIALS

- newspaper
- fresh black washable marker
- paper coffee filter
- cotton ball
- eyedropper
- rubbing alcohol
- small rubber band (Rainbow Loom bands work well)
- scissors

WHAT REALLY HAPPENED?

❋ Chromatography is a process used to separate parts of a solution that has different chemicals inside it. Ink is made of several different molecules, each with their own size and color. What colors did you find in the ink you used?

❋ Each molecule in the ink travels at a different speed when pulled along the piece of paper. The most lightweight particles move more quickly and over greater distances than the heavier particles, kind of like a race.

YOUR TURN TO EXPERIMENT

Try making chromatograms using other colors of markers. What colors appear on the chromatograms?

SPIDER ENGINEERING

Build a spiderweb like an arachnid.

When spiders abandon their old webs, cobwebs linger in corners and near the ceiling, collecting dirt and dust. In Minecraft, these old webs slow things down. **SPIDERS ARE AMAZINGLY SKILLED ARCHITECTS,** making their webs with lots of details and artistic patterns. Do you have the skills necessary to build a web as beautiful as a real spider web?

INSTRUCTIONS

1. Find an image of a spiderweb online or find one in real life.

2. Tie one end of the dental floss to one branch of the stick.

3. Pretend you are a spider and weave a web that looks like the real thing. Move the floss in repeating patterns and cross over the center of your web again and again.

WHAT REALLY HAPPENED?

✳ Spiders make their webs out of silk, which is a special protein they produce. They make silk in a part of their body called a gland and use their legs to pull it out. This is called spinning.

✳ Spiders spin webs to catch insects for food.

✳ The strongest silk is made by the golden orb spider. This spider's silk is stronger than steel, and fifty times lighter!

REAL-LIFE CONNECTIONS

Go on a spiderweb hunt. Take a walk through the woods, carefully looking for spiderwebs. Draw any that you see here.

CRACK THE CODE

Use binary code to solve a riddle.

Binary code is how computers talk and represent information. **BINARY CODE is a TWO-NUMBER SYSTEM**, which means it uses only two numbers to make a code for all the information in a computer. Those numbers are 1 and 0. Everything you see on the computer (letters, numbers, and pictures) is made up of different **COMBINATIONS OF 1s AND 0s**. In this activity, you get to use computer code to solve a question!

INSTRUCTIONS

Take a look at the binary code alphabet below. It shows the computer code for each letter. This is how computers represent each letter of the alphabet. Use the chart to figure out the answer to the riddle.

A	0 1 0 0 0 0 0 1		N	0 1 0 0 1 1 1 0
B	0 1 0 0 0 0 1 0		O	0 1 0 0 1 1 1 1
C	0 1 0 0 0 0 1 1		P	0 1 0 1 0 0 0 0
D	0 1 0 0 0 1 0 0		Q	0 1 0 1 0 0 0 1
E	0 1 0 0 0 1 0 1		R	0 1 0 1 0 0 1 0
F	0 1 0 0 0 1 1 0		S	0 1 0 1 0 0 1 1
G	0 1 0 0 0 1 1 1		T	0 1 0 1 0 1 0 0
H	0 1 0 0 1 0 0 0		U	0 1 0 1 0 1 0 1
I	0 1 0 0 1 0 0 1		V	0 1 0 1 0 1 1 0
J	0 1 0 0 1 0 1 0		W	0 1 0 1 0 1 1 1
K	0 1 0 0 1 0 1 1		X	0 1 0 1 1 0 0 0
L	0 1 0 0 1 1 0 0		Y	0 1 0 1 1 0 0 1
M	0 1 0 0 1 1 0 1		Z	0 1 0 1 1 0 1 0

I TAKE JUST FOUR SECONDS TO EXPLODE WHEN ACTIVATED BY REDSTONE. WHAT AM I?

01010100	01001110	01010100

ACTIVATING END RODS
Discover how temperature affects glow sticks.

Travel bravely to the End and you'll probably notice **END RODS**, lighted sticks that naturally generate there. End rods are used in Minecraft for lighting and decoration, just like real-world glow sticks. Have you ever wondered why you need to **BEND A GLOW STICK** to make it light up? If so, prepare to be enLIGHTened.

INSTRUCTIONS

1. Before beginning this activity, feel the glow stick. How warm or cold does it feel? Write your observations on the chart.

2. Fill one glass cup with ice water.

3. Have a parent fill the second glass cup with very hot water (almost boiling).

4. Break one glow stick and observe the temperature again.

5. Break the second glow stick and shake both sticks to activate them completely.

6. At the same time, drop one glow stick into the ice water and one into the hot water.

7. Turn off the lights and watch. Jot down your observations on the chart below.

Observation Chart

Glow sticks before experiment	Glow sticks after breaking	Glow stick in ice water	Glow stick in hot water

TIME
10 minutes

MATERIALS
- 2 glow sticks of the same color
- 2 glass cups or jars
- ice water
- hot water

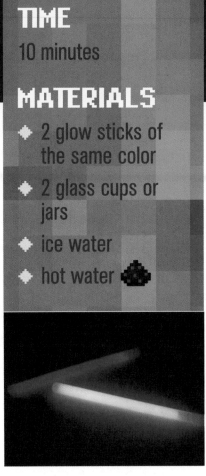

WHAT REALLY HAPPENED?

❋ When you bend the glow stick, a thin glass tube inside it breaks and releases a chemical. This chemical mixes with another chemical inside the larger plastic tube. When these two chemicals mix, light is produced. This is called **CHEMILUMINESCENCE.**

❋ Chemiluminescence does not produce any heat. You probably observed that the temperature of the glow stick was the same as the air around you and that its temperature did not change after it was activated.

❋ Chemical reactions happen at a faster rate with heat and are slowed down when cooled. The glow stick in the hot water should have glowed more brightly because the reaction was happening at a faster rate.

YOUR TURN TO EXPERIMENT

All glow sticks lose their glow after a few hours. Try putting one glow stick in the refrigerator or the freezer and the other glow stick in a warm place. Which glow stick stays bright the longest?

FLOWER PIGMENT POWER

Use natural pigments to make colorful art.

Young Minecrafters love using dyes to change the color of sheep in Minecraft. Gamers can also use Minecrafting resources like cocoa beans, cacti, and dandelions to **CREATE DYES** that change the color of armor, wolf collars, and shulkers. Nature provides an incredible variety of colors for us to use as pigments. Humans have used **PLANT PIGMENTS** for thousands of years to change the color of fabric, hair, and even skin. In this activity, you'll use the **FOOD AND PLANT RESOURCES** in your own kitchen and backyard to make fabric art.

INSTRUCTIONS

1. Cut the fabric to the desired size of the finished product. (If you plan to frame your cloth, allow space around the edge to wrap the fabric around the cardboard in the frame.)

2. Gather the plant products you intend to use as pigments. Cut the flowers from the stems. If using berries, smash them to release the juices.

3. Choose an area that can be safely pounded with a hammer. Sidewalks and driveways work well. If necessary, cover the work surface with newspaper to prevent staining.

4. Lay a piece of wax paper slightly larger than the cloth on the work surface. Then place the cloth on top.

5. When you are ready to begin, place flowers and leaves face down on the fabric. Add berry juices, coffee grounds, or vegetable parts in their desired locations.

6. Cover the fabric and plants with a second piece of wax paper.

7. Put on your eye protection. Carefully hammer the wax paper to transfer the plant pigments onto the fabric.

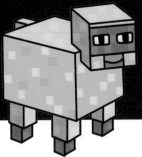

8. Remove the fabric and peel away the objects.

9. Rinse the fabric in cold water. Note: The pigments may fade after being washed.

WHAT REALLY HAPPENED

✳ Scientists believe that humans have been using plant pigments since the days of cave paintings way back in 15,000 BC. Egyptians dyed fibers starting in 2000 BC.

✳ Most plants contain a lot of different pigments. Pigments help plants stay alive and help us add color where we want it! The green pigment in a plant is called chlorophyll. It helps absorb energy from the sun to make food. Bright pigments in plants and fruit attract insects (like bees) that help plants reproduce.

YOUR TURN TO EXPERIMENT

Try dyeing different kinds of paper and fabric to see which one holds the color best. Make a chart to record what happens.

TIME

20 minutes–1 hour

MATERIALS

◆ white or light-colored cotton fabric (for example, cloth napkins, rags, pillowcases)

◆ scissors

◆ plants and food items to use as pigments:

   coffee grounds

   fresh beets, thinly sliced—caution: may stain

   berries

   flower petals

   cabbage leaves

   tea bags

◆ wax paper

◆ eye protection

◆ hammer

STEM QUEST MATH MINUTE 1

Sharpen your math skills while you craft.

Numbers and adding are important in Minecraft when you need to gather enough ingredients in your inventory to make weapons, armor, food, tools, and much more. Use the **MINECRAFTING RECIPES** here to practice your math. Calculate the total number of items needed. Write your answers next to Items Total.

TNT

    5 gunpowder
+ 4 blocks of sand
_____
    items total

Bow

    3 sticks
+ 3 pieces of string
_____
    items total

Arrows

    1 stick
    1 feather
+ 1 flint
_____
    items total

Enchantment Table

    4 obsidian blocks
    2 diamonds
+ 1 book
_____
    items total

Wood Pickaxe

    2 sticks
+ 3 wood planks
_____
    items total

Bed

    3 blocks of wool
+ 3 planks
_____
    items total

CRITICAL THINKING

Which ingredient is the most useful one based on
the recipes shown?

Which recipe requires the smallest number of items and the greatest
variety of items?

Write your own math formula for a new Minecraft weapon or tool below:

STORM MODELS

Recreate dramatic weather events.

TIME

5–20 minutes for each part

MATERIALS (RAIN)

- glass jar or cup
- water
- white, foamy shaving cream
- 2–3 food coloring choices
- small bowls or cups
- 2–3 eyedroppers

The sky darkens, villagers return to their homes, and Endermen teleport away as it starts to pour. Storms occur in Minecraft with just as much intensity as they do in the real world. **MAKE MODELS** of rain, snow, and thunder in this activity and learn more about **METEOROLOGY,** the science of weather.

INSTRUCTIONS FOR THE RAIN MODEL

1. Fill a glass jar or cup with water, leaving 2–3 inches at the top for shaving cream.
2. Use shaving cream to make a cloud on top of the water.
3. In separate bowls or cups, mix water and food coloring.
4. Using a separate eyedropper for each color, squirt colored water on top of the shaving cream cloud. Repeat the process with the other colors in separate areas of the cloud.
5. Watch as the cloud gets heavy with water and precipitates colored rain.

WHAT REALLY HAPPENED?

❋ Clouds form when water vapor rises into the air and condenses. When clouds become saturated with (full of) water, gravity pulls droplets toward the Earth, causing rain.

INSTRUCTIONS FOR THE THUNDER MODEL

1. Blow into a brown paper lunch bag.

2. Twist the end of the bag closed.

3. Quickly hit the bag with your other hand.

WHAT REALLY HAPPENED

❋ When you hit the bag, the air inside the bag compressed quickly. This caused the bag to break when the air rushed out. As the air from inside the bag rushed out, it pushed the air outside the bag away. The movement of the air created a sound wave, which you heard as a bang.

❋ Thunder is created when lightning passes from a cloud to the Earth. As the lightning moves toward the Earth, it separates the air. After the lightning passes, the air collapses back together and creates a sound wave, which we hear as thunder.

INSTRUCTIONS FOR THE SNOW MODEL

1. Place each diaper in the bowl and carefully cut the first layer of material. Remove the cotton from inside the diaper and set it aside.

2. Pour the powdery material from inside the diaper into the bowl. Repeat with the remaining diapers.

3. One ounce at a time, pour up to 4 ounces of water for each diaper used over the powder. Gently mix the powder and water with your fingers until it begins to thicken and form soft "snow."

4. Enjoy playing in the snow! How does this snow feel the same as or different from real snow?

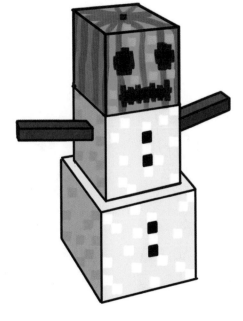

WHAT REALLY HAPPENED

❄ The tiny molecule chains that make up the material inside diapers expand when they are filled with water, just like sponges do. Some chains of molecules, called polymers, can soak up to 800 times their weight in water!

❄ Real snow forms when ice crystals in clouds stick together. When lots of ice crystals stick together, they become heavy enough to fall to the ground as snow.

COLOR-CREEPING CREEPER

Get an exciting look at capillary action.

Creepers are hostile mobs that sneak up on players, give off a short *hissss*, and then boom! **WATER** has special creeping abilities as well. Capillary action is water's superpower: it allows water to move in a way that **DEFIES GRAVITY.** Prepare to watch a creeper get its bright green color with the help of **CAPILLARY ACTION.**

INSTRUCTIONS

1. Fill the bowl with water and add several drops of green food coloring. Place it on a table lined with wax paper.

2. Cut the paper towel into a long, 2-inch strip.

3. Using the permanent marker, draw the outline of a creeper on one end of the paper towel strip.

4. Place the other end of the strip in the green water and extend the rest of the paper towel outside the bowl.

5. Let the creeping begin!

WHAT REALLY HAPPENED

✳ In this activity, water moves through the paper towel by a process called capillary action. Water molecules are attracted to the paper towel, but they are also attracted to each other. As one water molecule travels up the paper towel, it grabs another water molecule to pull along. The process continues until the water reaches the end of the paper towel. How do you think this makes paper towels good for cleaning spills?

MATERIALS
- medium to large bowl (glass works best)
- water
- green food coloring
- wax paper
- scissors
- paper towels (two connected sheets)
- black permanent marker

☀ Plants use capillary action to move water from their roots, up through their stems, into their leaves, and out into the air.

YOUR TURN TO EXPERIMENT

☀ **CELERY** can also change color through capillary action. Design an experiment with water and food coloring to see for yourself.

☀ Draw your experiment idea below:

SNOW GOLEM SHOOTER

Shooting projectiles and investigating force.

A snow golem, despite his scary appearance, can defend a player against hostile mobs by **THROWING** snowballs at enemies. He must be created by a player or randomly created by an Enderman. He moves around by sliding on a snow path he creates for himself. He can also supply **SNOWBALLS** on demand for players building igloos. In this activity, you'll create a snow golem that demonstrates how we can use **FORCE** to shoot pom-pom "snowballs" from pool noodles.

INSTRUCTIONS

1. Have a parent use the knife to cut the pool noodles into the following sizes:
   - One 3-inch piece of orange pool noodle

   - One 3-inch piece of white pool noodle

   - One 2-inch piece of white pool noodle

2. Use the scissors to cut about an inch off the open end of the balloon. Set aside.

2. Pull the open end of the balloon over the end of the 3-inch white noodle so that it fits snuggly and blocks the noodle hole on one side.

3. Snap two toothpicks in half to make four halves.

4. Stack the white noodle pieces so that the 2-inch white noodle is on the bottom and the open holes face forward and noodle ends are flush with each other. Use the toothpick halves to spear the two white noodle pieces together. (Add more toothpicks as needed.)

5. Set the orange noodle piece on the table with a hole pointing up and use the marker to draw a pumpkin face on one side. Draw buttons on the white noodles.

6. Using the other toothpick halves, join the pumpkin face to the larger white noodle piece so that the balloon extends out from the golem's back.

7. Use the 2 whole toothpicks as arms for the snow golem.

8. Stick the unused portion of balloon out of the top of the snow golem's head for a pumpkin stem decoration.

9. Insert a marshmallow (or other projectile) in the front of the center noodle. Pinch the balloon, pull it back gently, and let it go. A marshmallow should shoot out of your snow golem.

WHAT REALLY HAPPENED?

A force is a push or a pull on an object. The force you use to pull back the balloon will be transferred to the snowball. Pulling it back farther will create a greater force than pulling it back only partway.

YOUR TURN TO EXPERIMENT

What other objects can you shoot out of your snow golem? Which ones travel the greatest distance?

Make targets for your snowballs and have a competition with a friend.

MATERIALS

- serrated knife
- 2 pool noodles of different colors (orange and white)
- 1 (white) balloon
- scissors
- 4–6 toothpicks
- black permanent marker
- mini marshmallows or small white or silver pom-poms (they should fit inside the hole of the pool noodle)

FLUORESCENT PROTEIN TORCH

Make a torch that uses highlighter ink to emit light.

Torches are found in dark areas around Minecraft, providing light for the player. Here, make your own torch by turning milk into plastic and adding the ink from a highlighter to make it fluorescent (you will need a black light to see the fluorescence).

INSTRUCTIONS

1. Measure 1 cup of milk in a glass measuring cup. Microwave for 2 minutes. Have a parent help you remove the milk from the microwave; it will be hot.

2. In a separate bowl, measure 4 teaspoons of white vinegar and add 5–7 drops of food coloring.

3. Have an adult remove the ink from the highlighter and add it to the bowl containing the vinegar and food coloring.

4. Add the colored vinegar to the hot milk.

5. Stir with the spoon. The milk will curdle and form clumps.

6. Strain the milk through the cloth, collecting the clumps in the cloth. Discard the liquid.

7. Use the rubber band to turn the fabric into a pouch containing the milk clumps. Allow to cool for 20–30 minutes. This is your milk plastic.

8. While you wait, use the black marker to color the whole outside of the toilet paper roll.

8. When the milk plastic is cool enough to handle, unwrap the clumps and smush them together into the shape of a ball. Allow the ball to harden for 30–60 minutes.

9. Place the milk plastic ball on top of the toilet paper roll. After the milk plastic has completely dried and hardened (2–3 days), ask a grown-up to hot glue it to the toilet paper roll.

10. In a dark room lit with the black light, check out your torch.

WHAT REALLY HAPPENED?

❊ Black lights emit ultraviolet (UV) light, which we cannot see. Fluorescence is light given off by certain substances (like highlighter ink) when they absorb UV light. First the substance absorbs energy, and then it gives off light. The torch emits light thanks to its fluorescent highlighter ink.

YOUR TURN TO EXPERIMENT

❊ There are some animals that naturally fluoresce. Do some research to see which animals have the ability of biofluorescence and how this adaptation helps them survive in their habitat.

TIME

1 hour and 20 minutes (plus 2–3 days of hardening time)

MATERIALS

◆ 1 cup whole milk
◆ glass measuring cup
◆ small bowl
◆ 4 teaspoons of white vinegar
◆ yellow food coloring
◆ orange or yellow highlighter with liquid ink
◆ scrap of fabric or cheesecloth
◆ rubber band
◆ empty toilet paper roll
◆ black permanent marker
◆ black light
◆ hot glue gun

TALL TOWER ENGINEERING

Think like an engineer and build a tower that's tall and strong!

Minecraft is the perfect place to fine-tune your tower-building skills, but you are limited to **BUILDING STRUCTURES** that are 255 blocks high. In this activity, the only limits are based in **PHYSICS**. Experiment with different bases and shapes and think like an engineer to make a marshmallow skyscraper that's **STRONG AND STURDY** enough to last!

INSTRUCTIONS

1. Consider your strategy. Before you begin building, figure out which shapes you can make with toothpicks and marshmallows. Which one will make the strongest base? (Wobble them to find out.)

2. Using what you learned about the strengths of the shapes, build the tallest, free-standing (not touching anything) tower you can imagine. Use the cutting board or cookie sheet for a solid foundation.

3. Measure your tower and record the height below.

DATA

Make a sketch of your designs below, then measure and record the height of each.

Trial 1:	Trial 2:
Height:	Height:

TIME

30 minutes

MATERIALS

◆ bag of miniature marshmallows (leave open overnight so they're stale)

◆ box of at least 100 toothpicks

◆ cutting board or cookie sheet

◆ tape measure, ruler, or meter/yardstick

WHAT REALLY HAPPENED?

※ An engineer is a person who designs and builds complex machines and structures. The process you used to create your tall tower is very similar to the way engineers think about problems and design solutions. This method of problem-solving is called the **ENGINEERING DESIGN PROCESS.**

※ Different shapes have different strengths. Triangles make a strong base, which is why they are often used by builders.

YOUR TURN TO EXPERIMENT

※ Do some research to find out which shapes engineers use to build really tall towers and really long bridges. Find photos of famous tall buildings online and see if you can copy the design with marshmallows and toothpicks.

※ Challenge your parents, siblings, or friends to build a tower taller than yours. Who can build the tallest free-standing tower with marshmallows and toothpicks?

BIOME ENGINEERING
Build a biome and watch it grow.

A biome is an **ECOLOGICAL COMMUNITY**, like a rainforest, desert, or grassland. The natural world has a total of fourteen biomes (five aquatic and nine land biomes). There are sixty-two different biomes in Minecraft. Try building your own biome—either based in **NATURE** or similar to one in Minecraft. You could even come up with your very own biome and give it a name!

INSTRUCTIONS

1. Place a 1-inch layer of gravel on the bottom of the container.

2. Place a 1-inch layer of sand over the gravel.

3. Mix 2 cups of soil and 1 cup of sand. Place a 2–3 inch layer of the sand/soil mixture over the gravel. (For desert biomes, mix ½ cup of soil with 3 cups of sand.)

4. Plant the plants in the soil. (If using seeds, allow time for them to sprout.)

5. Add small critters, if you choose.

6. Gently add water until you see a small amount of water in the bottom of the tank.

7. Place the biome in a sunny location and add water when needed.

WHAT REALLY HAPPENED?

❋ Biomes are large geographical areas with specific climates, plants, and animals.

❋ The biosphere is the part of the Earth's atmosphere that supports life. It includes both living and nonliving things.

❋ Engineers call artificial environments (ones made by people) biodomes. A biodome is a model that is designed to represent a particular environment and the organisms that live there. You created one!

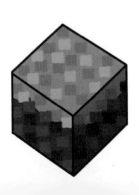

YOUR TURN TO EXPERIMENT

❋ Experiment with your biome. Change the amounts of substrate or the depth of the layers. Make a few different biomes and change the amount of light and water they get. What are the best conditions for your biome?

❋ Try making a self-sufficient environment by putting a lid on your biome. If it succeeds, you won't need to water your biome because the water will recycle itself. You will be able to watch the water cycle in action!

❋ Design a new biome! Research to find out which plants and animals can live together.

CHARGED CREEPER
Repurpose and rewire a motor.

Creepers are scary enough to begin with, but **CHARGED CREEPERS** are even more deadly! Charged by a lightning strike, this kind of creeper has a glowing blue aura and twice the **EXPLOSIVE POWER.** You can make your own charged creeper by upcycling a vibrating toothbrush motor and retrofitting it with a new battery. **WATCH IT GO!**

INSTRUCTIONS

1. With help from a grown-up, break open the toothbrush and remove the motor and battery. You may need to use pliers. Be careful not to damage the wires.

2. Observe how the motor works by turning the switch on and off. Experiment with the circuit by taking wires on and off the ends of the battery and switching them around to understand how they work.

3. Remove the old battery and insert the watch battery. You may need to use electrical tape to keep the metal ends of the wires attached to the smaller battery. You can also use aluminum foil to close any gaps that may have formed.

4. Cut a small section out of one end of the pool noodle as needed so that the motor and battery can be placed inside. Use clear packing tape to keep the battery tucked up inside the pool noodle with the motor sticking out of the noodle.

5. Use the permanent marker to draw a creeper on the pool noodle. (The head should be at the end opposite the battery.)

6. Turn on the motor, sit the creeper up with the motor on the table or floor, and watch your charged creeper vibrate across the surface.

WHAT REALLY HAPPENED?

❇ A circuit is a path that allows electricity to flow. Materials that allow electric current to pass through them easily are called conductors. Conductors can be used to link the positive and negative ends of a battery, forming a circuit.

❇ If you experimented with the wires on the battery, you noticed that the battery had to be connected at the positive end and the negative end. If one end is not connected, energy cannot flow and power the device.

YOUR TURN TO EXPERIMENT

What other inventions could you make from a toothbrush motor and battery?

Have a charged **CREEPER DANCE PARTY.** Invite some friends to make charged creepers with you and allow them to dance around on the floor together. Is there any way to control which way the charged creepers move?

TIME
1 hour

MATERIALS
◆ vibrating toothbrush (used or new)
◆ pliers
◆ watch battery (3-volt battery)
◆ electrical tape
◆ aluminum foil
◆ 4 inches of green pool noodle
◆ clear packing tape
◆ black permanent marker
◆ knife

STEM QUEST
MATH MINUTE 2

These problems use wordplay instead of swordplay.

Minecrafters love to joke around and have fun. Have you heard these jokes? Find the solution to the math problems at right and then use the key below to fill in the punch lines.

KEY

A	B	C	D	E	F
2	9	16	12	5	11

G	H	I	J	K	L
20	19	26	23	13	8

M	N	O	P	Q	R
6	18	10	4	3	15

S	T	U	V	W	X
21	7	17	1	25	22

Y	Z
24	14

1. WHAT IS A CREEPER'S FAVORITE COLOR?

4 +5	4 +4	2 +3	21 +4
Letter			

2. WHAT IS A WITCH'S FAVORITE SUBJECT IN SCHOOL?

15 +6	1 +3	0 +5	1 +7	3 +5	18 +8	11 +7	3 +17
Letter							

DIG IN

Mine for resources like a pro!

As any Minecrafter knows, mining is essential to surviving the game. Players have to dig into their world's **NATURAL RESOURCES** to gather different types of **STONE, METALS, WOOD, AND ORE.** Without these materials, players cannot build or create structures. In the real world, mining for resources is a difficult task. Resources have to be located, **EXTRACTED FROM THE EARTH** without damaging the landscape, and then changed to new forms to be useful. See if you're up for the challenge of a real miner in this dig-and-discover activity.

INSTRUCTIONS

1. Ask a friend or parent to fill the bottom of the container with one color of craft sand. Add several resources to the sand. Add a second layer of sand in a contrasting color and then add the remaining resources. Top with the third layer of sand to hide all the resources.

2. Observe the layers of sand by looking at the side of the container. The layers of sand represent the layers of soil and rock in the earth. Your goal is to remove the resources while not disturbing the layers of sand.

3. Use colored pencils, crayons, or markers to draw the layers of sand in the top box at right.

4. Ask a friend to set the stopwatch for 60 seconds, which will represent one day of mining.

5. When your friend says go, you will have 60 seconds to very carefully remove as many resources as possible using your tools. Remember, your goal is to remove the resources with as little change as possible to the sand layers.

6. After your 60-second "day," record the number of resources you found on the table on page 92.

7. Repeat Steps 3–5 until all the resources have been mined.

8. Draw the layers of sand in the bottom box at right after you finish mining.

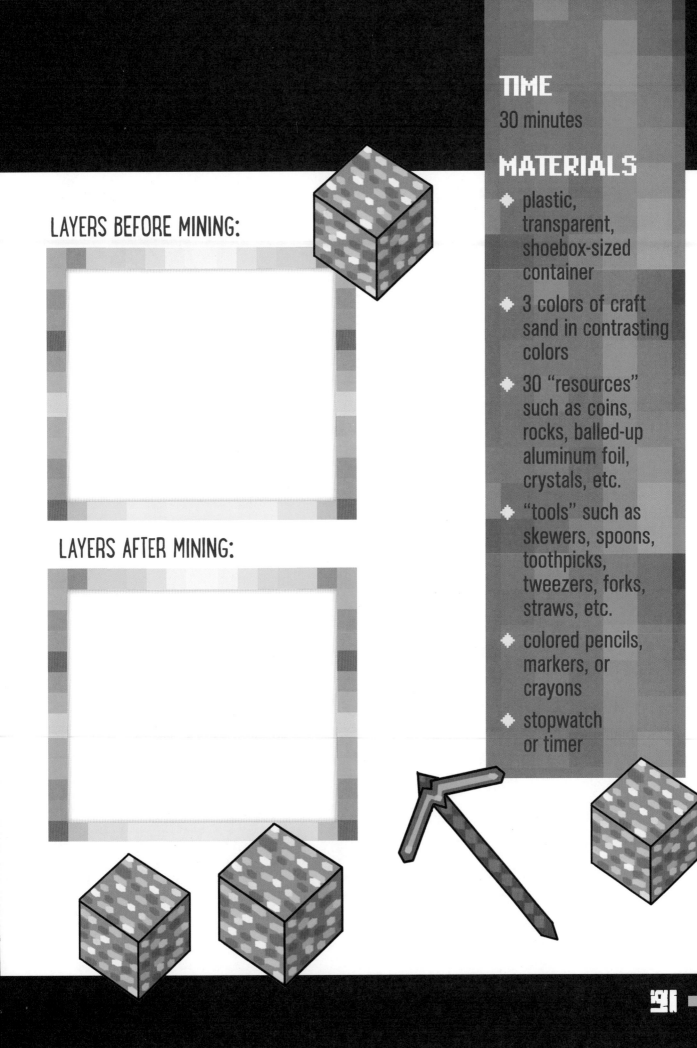

LAYERS BEFORE MINING:

LAYERS AFTER MINING:

TIME

30 minutes

MATERIALS

- plastic, transparent, shoebox-sized container

- 3 colors of craft sand in contrasting colors

- 30 "resources" such as coins, rocks, balled-up aluminum foil, crystals, etc.

- "tools" such as skewers, spoons, toothpicks, tweezers, forks, straws, etc.

- colored pencils, markers, or crayons

- stopwatch or timer

RECORD THE NUMBER OF RESOURCES YOU MINED EACH DAY:

Time	Number of Resources
Day 1	
Day 2	
Day 3	
Day 4	
Day 5	
Day 6	
Day 7	

WHAT REALLY HAPPENED?

❋ Miners dig into the Earth to remove natural resources. Natural resources are items that we can use, such as coal or gold.

❋ Earth has lots of resources, but it takes a long time for them to form. Just like in this activity, as more and more resources are removed by mining, it becomes harder to find more of the same.

❋ Mining can be disruptive to the environment. Land must be cleared, but digging into the Earth can disrupt plants and animals that live there.

❋ Scientists are looking for new ways to remove resources to protect the environment. They are also looking for new ways to make things that will require less mining. Do you have any ideas?

YOUR TURN TO EXPERIMENT

Draw or create a brand new machine or tool that will help find resources and protect the soil.

MATH FOR MINECRAFTERS

COUNTING NUMBERS

Connect the dots to keep this snow golem from melting. Count out loud as you go!

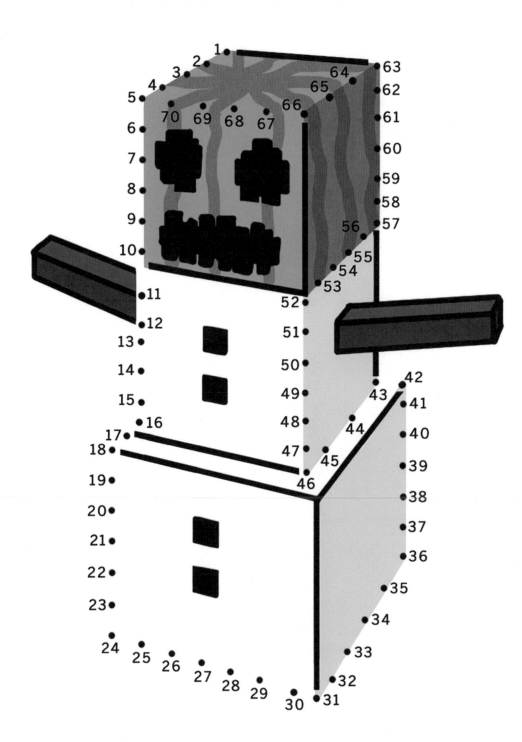

NUMBERS TO 100

Help the villager count the blocks. Fill in the missing numbers.

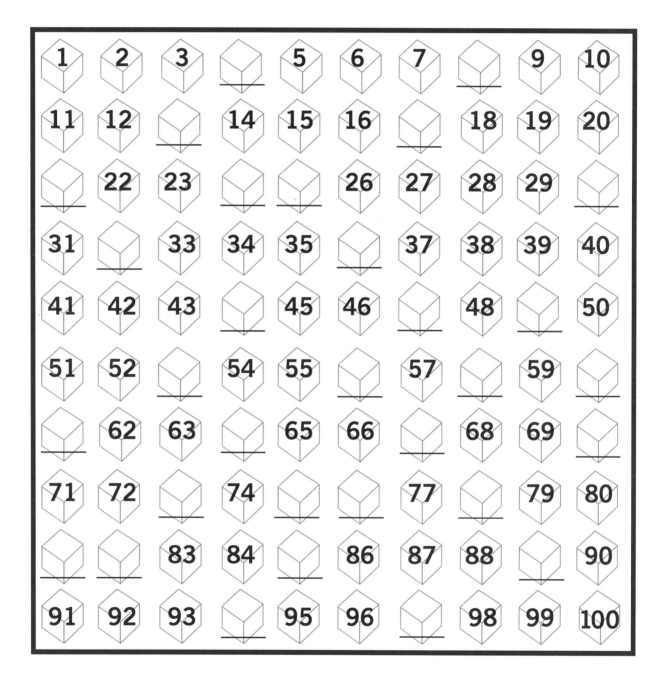

1	2	3		5	6	7		9	10
11	12		14	15	16		18	19	20
	22	23			26	27	28	29	
31		33	34	35		37	38	39	40
41	42	43		45	46		48		50
51	52		54	55		57		59	
	62	63		65	66		68	69	
71	72		74			77		79	80
		83	84		86	87	88		90
91	92	93		95	96		98	99	100

ODD AND EVEN NUMBERS

Use the chart to color the numbers and identify two dangerous mobs.

Odd Numbers 0 to 10 – Gray
Even Numbers 0 to 10 – Black

Odd Numbers 11 to 50 – Green
Even Numbers 11 to 50 – Pink

3	45	7	27	33	17	15	21
23	2	4	11	29	2	4	49
15	6	8	19	27	6	8	33
23	17	25	2	4	31	45	47
37	35	43	6	8	29	37	19
21	4	6	8	2	4	6	15
39	2	41	17	27	43	8	13
49	11	15	35	13	17	37	49

Name this dangerous mob.

_____

3	5	33	41	24	28	40	22
1	7	9	27	26	42	28	14
5	2		13	30	4		36
7	3	11	5	9	32	44	18
9	5	17	1	7	12	42	20
3	7	25	12	16	24	14	48
1	5	31	14	20	34	32	18
5	3	35	49	13	15	27	33

Name this dangerous mob.

_____

COUNT BY TWO

The mushrooms in the forest are growing by twos. Help the witch count the mushrooms.

_____   _____

_____   _____   _____

_____   _____   _____

COUNT BY THREE

The withers are attacking! Count by threes to count how many heads.

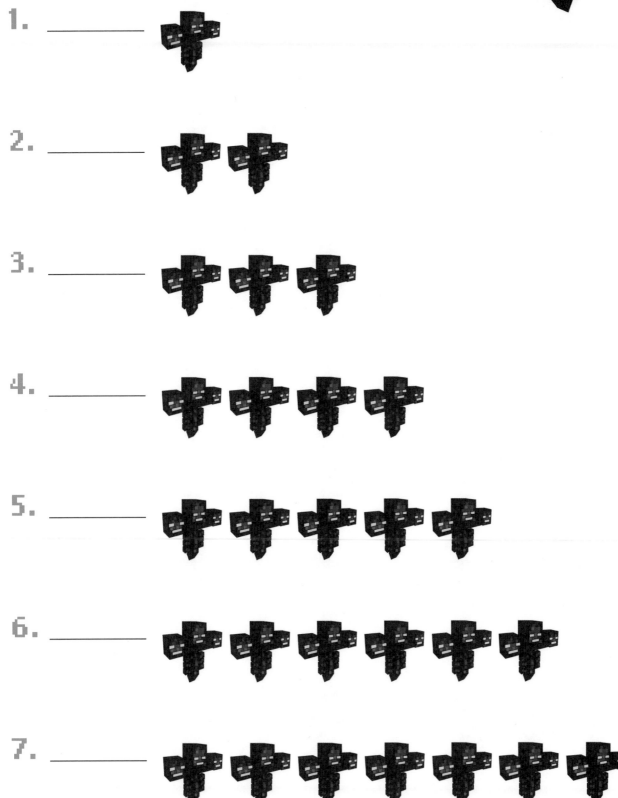

1. _____

2. _____

3. _____

4. _____

5. _____

6. _____

7. _____

COUNT BY FIVE

The creepers are planning a big explosion! They have placed the TNT blocks into stacks of five. Count the stacks to find out how many TNT blocks they plan to blow.

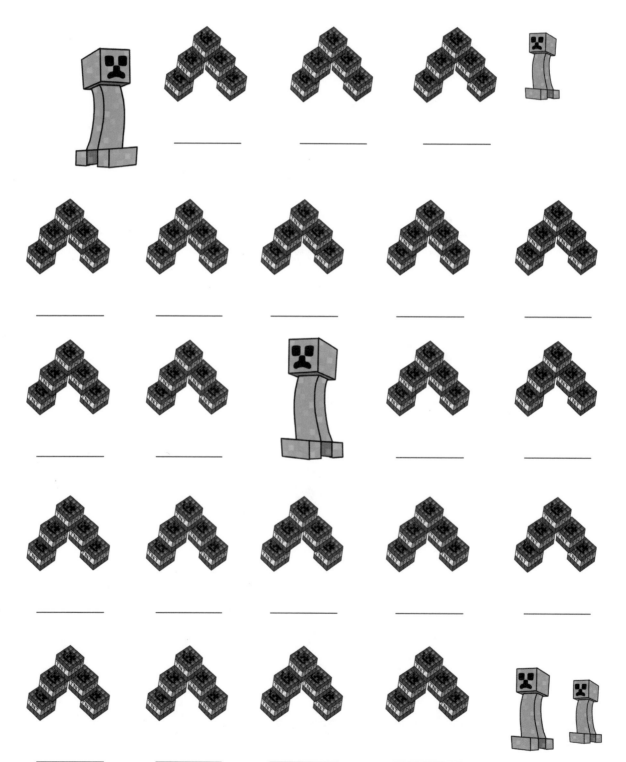

_____ _____ _____

_____ _____ _____ _____ _____

_____ _____ _____ _____

_____ _____ _____ _____

COUNT BY 10

The zombies are coming in groups of 10. Count by tens to see how many zombies are attacking.

_____   _____   _____

_____   _____   _____

_____   _____   _____

WHAT COMES NEXT?

Look at the pattern. Circle the picture that continues the pattern.

WHAT COMES NEXT?

Look at the pattern. Draw the next picture to continue the pattern.

1.

2.

3.

4.

5.

COMPARING NUMBERS

Use <, >, or = to compare the numbers.

Add the numbers. Then compare.

1. $3+4$ ☐ $2+5$

2. $7+2$ ☐ $3+5$

3. $2+6$ ☐ $6+3$

4. $1+8$ ☐ $4+5$

5. $4+2$ ☐ $3+5$

6. $5+2$ ☐ $2+3$

7. $1+2$ ☐ $1+1$

8. $3+3$ ☐ $4+4$

9. $7+1$ ☐ $5+3$

10. $4+0$ ☐ $0+5$

11. $5+2$ ☐ $8+1$

12. $4+4$ ☐ $5+4$

MATH ON THE FARM

Read the problem. Draw a picture to solve.

1. Alex collects 6 eggs on Monday and 3 eggs on Tuesday. How many eggs does she collect in all? _____

2. Horse ate 2 carrots in the morning. It ate 4 carrots at night. How many carrots did it eat in all? _____

3. There are 3 pigs and 4 baby pigs in the pen. How many pigs are there in all? _____

4. There are 5 sheep in the field and 3 sheep in the barn. How many sheep in all? _____

SUBTRACTING

Solve each problem. Use the answer to solve the riddle.

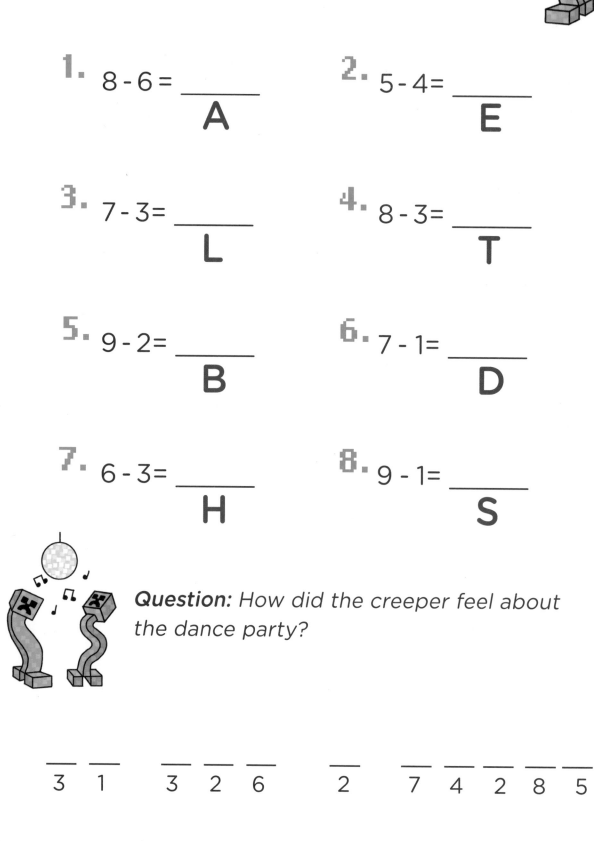

1. 8 - 6 = _____
   A

2. 5 - 4 = _____
   E

3. 7 - 3 = _____
   L

4. 8 - 3 = _____
   T

5. 9 - 2 = _____
   B

6. 7 - 1 = _____
   D

7. 6 - 3 = _____
   H

8. 9 - 1 = _____
   S

Question: How did the creeper feel about the dance party?

___ ___   ___ ___ ___   ___   ___ ___ ___ ___ ___ !
 3   1   3   2   6   2   7   4   2   8   5

MORE MATH ON THE FARM

Read the problem. Draw a picture to solve.

1. The chickens have 8 eggs, but 3 of them break. How many eggs are left? _____

2. Horse has 6 carrots. It eats 2 carrots. How many carrots are left? _____

3. There are 5 pigs on the farm. 2 become pork chops. How many pigs are left? _____

4. There are 7 rabbits on the farm. Suddenly, 4 rabbits hopped away. How many rabbits are left?

    _____

MISSING DOTS

Draw the missing dots to add up to the number shown.

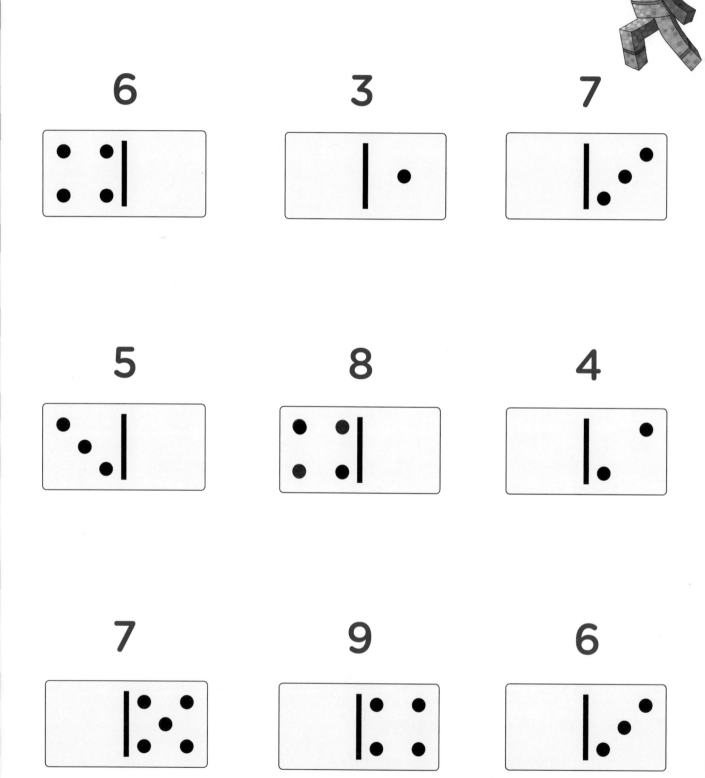

6

3

7

5

8

4

7

9

6

WHAT'S MISSING?

Draw the missing hearts to add up to the number on the top of the box. Then write how many hearts you drew.

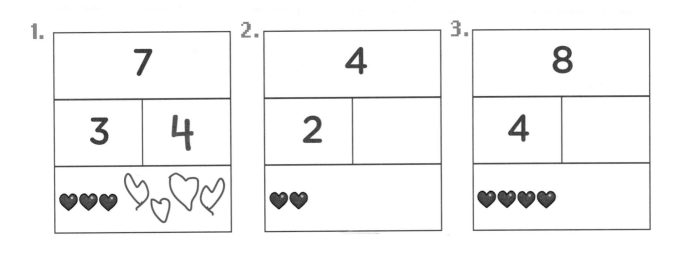

1.

7	
3	4

2.

4	
2	

3.

8	
4	

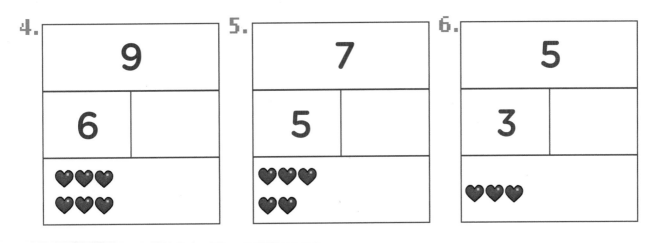

4.

9	
6	

5.

7	
5	

6.

5	
3	

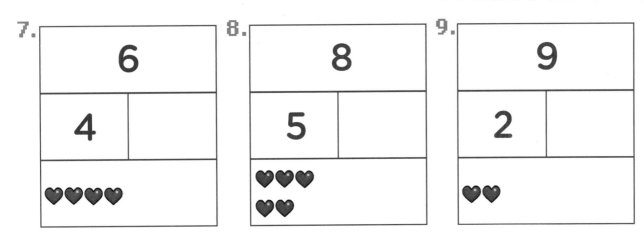

7.

6	
4	

8.

8	
5	

9.

9	
2	

MAKING 10

Color in the blank boxes. Write down how many boxes you colored to finish the addition problem.

1.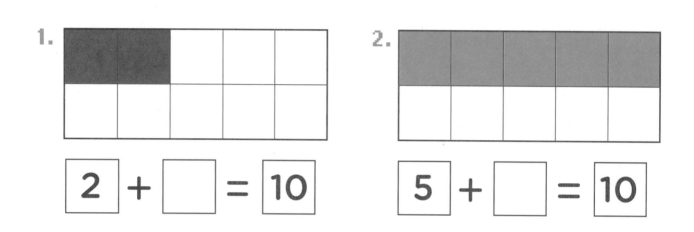

$$2 + \boxed{} = \boxed{10}$$

2.

$$5 + \boxed{} = \boxed{10}$$

3.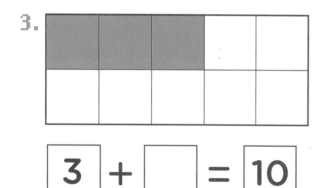

$$3 + \boxed{} = \boxed{10}$$

4.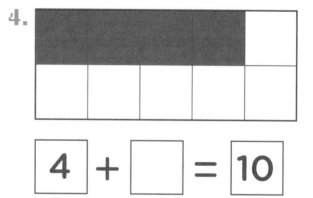

$$4 + \boxed{} = \boxed{10}$$

5.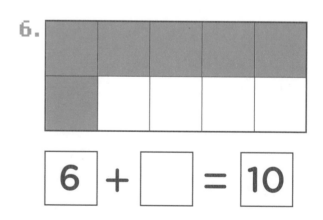

$$7 + \boxed{} = \boxed{10}$$

6.

$$6 + \boxed{} = \boxed{10}$$

TOWERS OF 10

Count how many blue and red blocks make up each tower of 10.

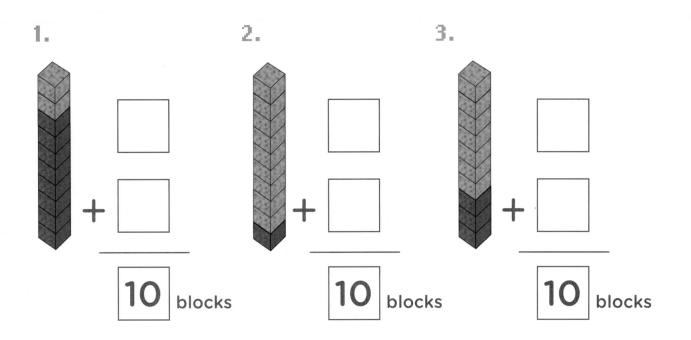

1.

☐ + ☐ ____ $\boxed{10}$ blocks

2.

☐ + ☐ ____ $\boxed{10}$ blocks

3.

☐ + ☐ ____ $\boxed{10}$ blocks

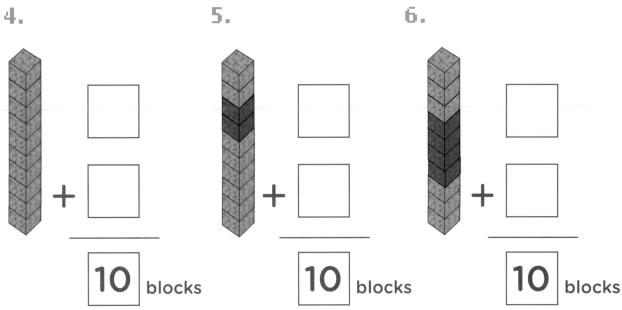

4.

☐ + ☐ ____ $\boxed{10}$ blocks

5.

☐ + ☐ ____ $\boxed{10}$ blocks

6.

☐ + ☐ ____ $\boxed{10}$ blocks

HOW MANY BLOCKS?

Count the towers of 10 and the blocks.

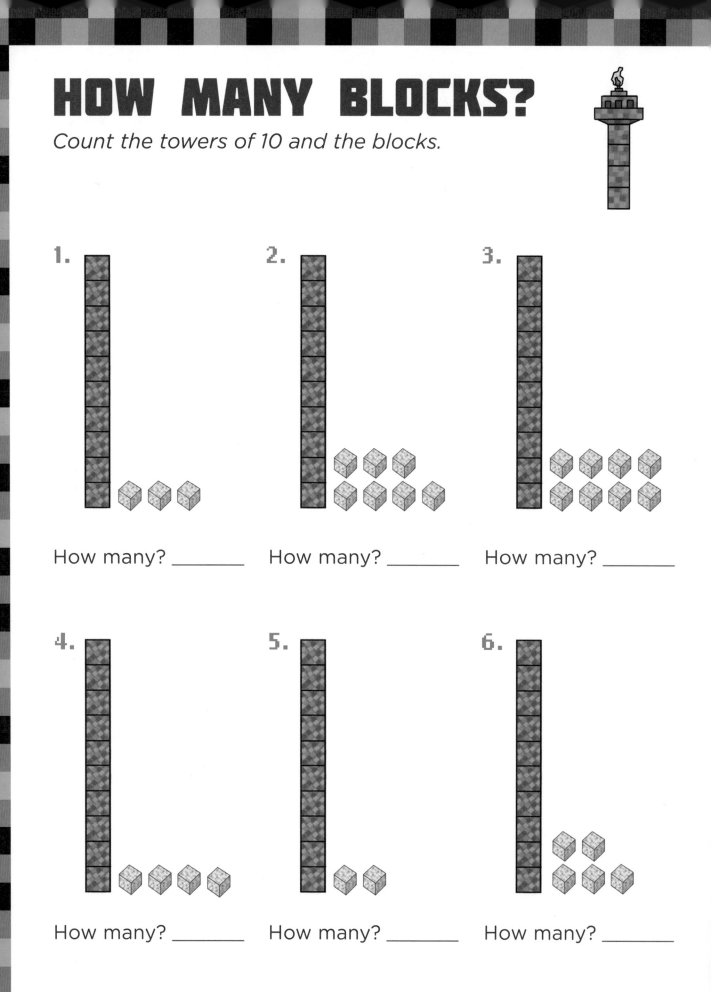

1.

How many? _____

2.

How many? _____

3.

How many? _____

4.

How many? _____

5.

How many? _____

6.

How many? _____

PLACE VALUE

Color the blocks to show how many tens and ones make up each number. The first one is done for you.

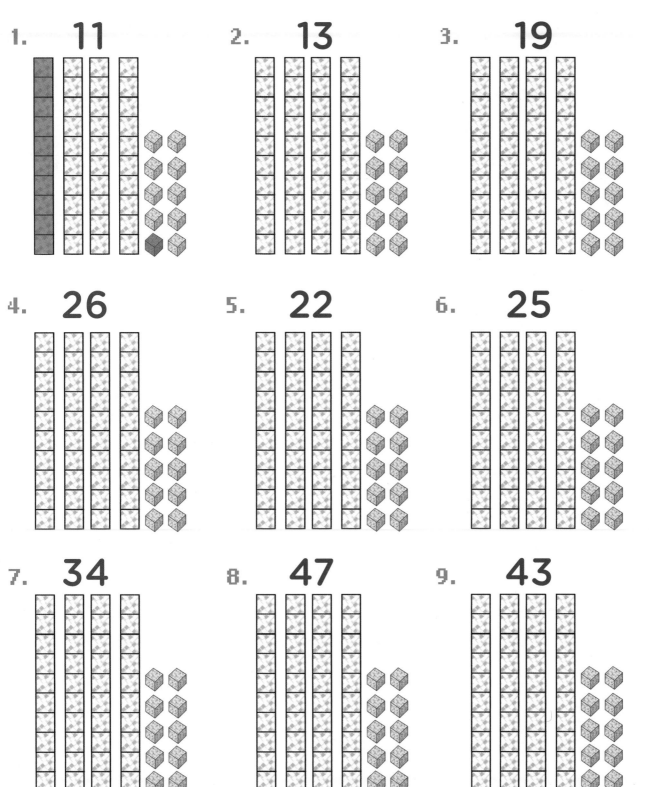

1. **11**

2. **13**

3. **19**

4. **26**

5. **22**

6. **25**

7. **34**

8. **47**

9. **43**

PLACE VALUE

Look at the number. Write how many tens and how many ones.

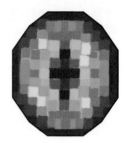

1.

52	
Tens	Ones

2.

37	
Tens	Ones

3.

24	
Tens	Ones

4.

16	
Tens	Ones

5.

20	
Tens	Ones

6.

41	
Tens	Ones

7.

52	
Tens	Ones

8.

93	
Tens	Ones

9.

75	
Tens	Ones

PLACE VALUE

Look at the number. Write how many tens and how many ones.

1.
82	
Tens	Ones

2.
56	
Tens	Ones

3.
70	
Tens	Ones

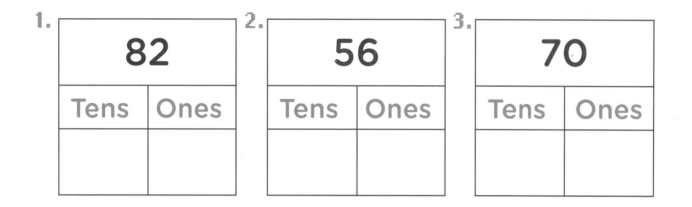

4.
61	
Tens	Ones

5.
12	
Tens	Ones

6.
79	
Tens	Ones

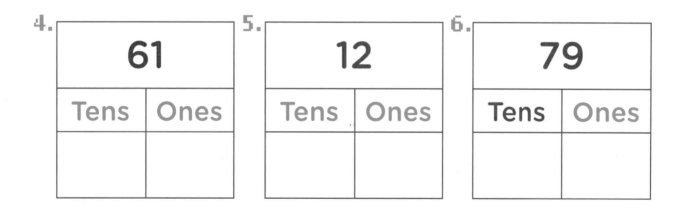

7.
95	
Tens	Ones

8.
26	
Tens	Ones

9.
33	
Tens	Ones

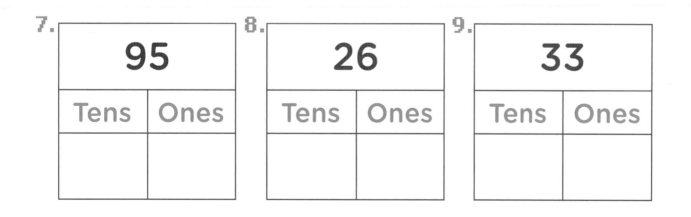

FACT FAMILIES

Look at the fact families. Then fill in the missing numbers.

1.

7

3   4

3 + 4 = _____

4 + _____ = 7

7 – 3 = _____

7 – 4 = _____

2.

6

1   5

5 + _____ = 6

1 + 5 = _____

6 – 1 = _____

6 – _____ = 1

3.

8

2   6

_____ + 6 = 8

2 + 6 = _____

8 – 2 = _____

_____ – 6 = 2

4.

9

2   7

7 + 2 = _____

2 + _____ = 9

9 – 7 = _____

9 – 2 = _____

ADDITION AND SUBTRACTION

Use what is known to solve the unknown.

1. I know **3 + 8 = 11,**
so I know . . .

8 + 3 = _____

11 − 3 = _____

11 − 8 = _____

2. I know **4 + 5 = 9,**
so I know . . .

5 + 4 = _____

9 − 4 = _____

9 − 5 = _____

3. I know **6 + 7 = 13,**
so I know . . .

7 + 6 = _____

13 − 6 = _____

13 − 7 = _____

4. I know **8 + 4 = 12,**
so I know . . .

4 + 8 = _____

12 − 8 = _____

12 − 4 = _____

TEN MORE

Look at the first number. Add ten in your head. Write the new number.

Adding 10 more in my head makes me feel smart!

1. | 20 | 30 |

2. | 50 | |

3. | 30 | |

4. | 44 | |

5. | 62 | |

6. | 71 | |

7. | 15 | |

8. | 36 | |

TEN MORE

Look at the first number. Add ten in your head.
Write the new number.

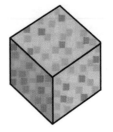

1.

| 30 | 40 |

2.

| 60 | |

3.

| 50 | |

4.

| 43 | |

5.

| 72 | |

6.

| 16 | |

7.

| 27 | |

8.

| 81 | |

SHAPES

Trace each shape. Draw your own in the boxes below.

triangle　　　**square**　　　**rectangle**　　　**trapezoid**

1.

2.

triangle

square

3.

4.

rectangle

trapezoid

SHAPE SHIFTER

Look at each shape. Then complete the chart.

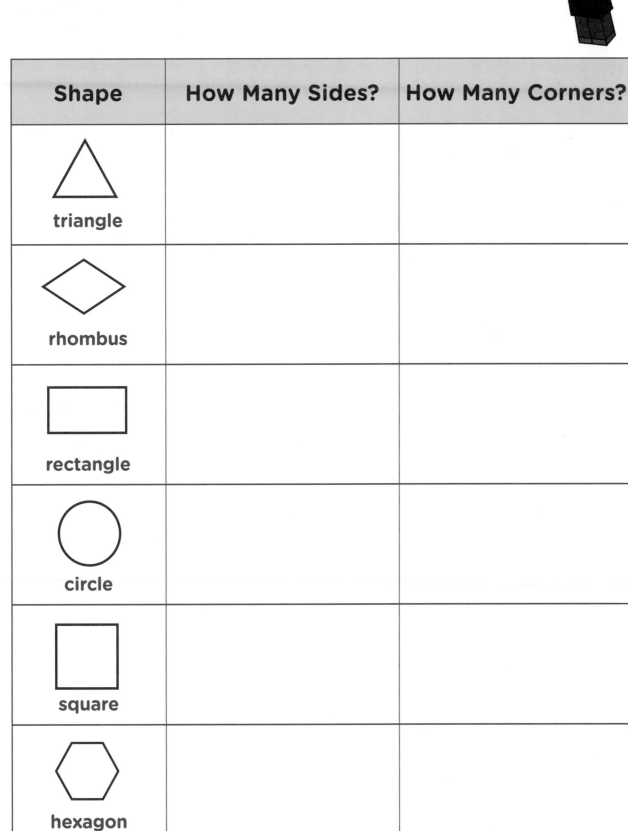

Shape	How Many Sides?	How Many Corners?
triangle		
rhombus		
rectangle		
circle		
square		
hexagon		

SHAPE UP!

Follow the directions to help Steve learn about shapes.

Squares look the same upside down!

1. Color the squares red.

2. Color the rectangles blue.

3. Color the triangles green.

4. Color the circles yellow.

ZOMBIE SHAPE INVASION

The Minecraft world is filled with squares and rectangles like you see in this zombie. Imagine that Minecraft was created with circles and ovals, triangles, and shapes with more than four sides. Draw what the zombie would look like in these imaginary Minecraft worlds.

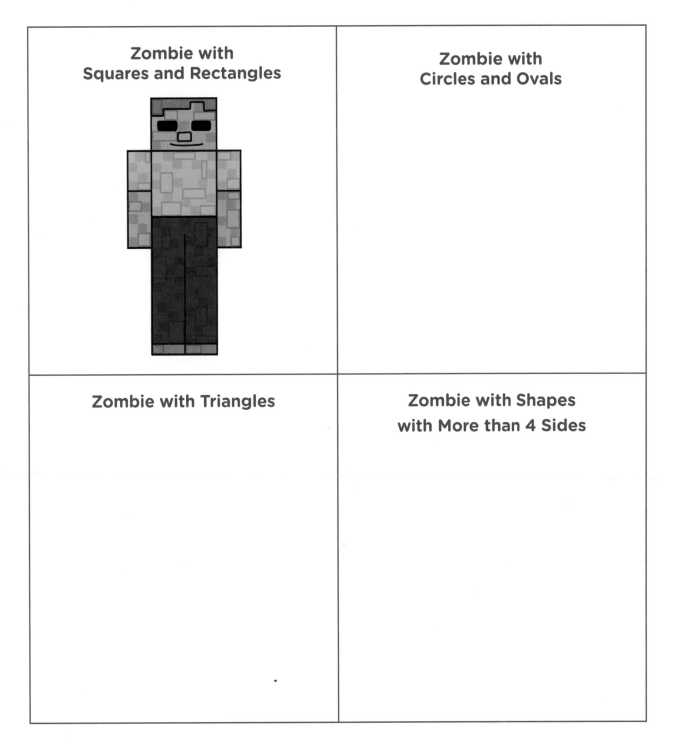

Zombie with Squares and Rectangles

Zombie with Circles and Ovals

Zombie with Triangles

Zombie with Shapes with More than 4 Sides

TELLING TIME

Look at the clocks. Write the time.

1.

____ : ____

2.

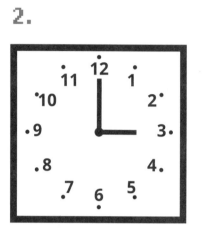

____ : ____

3.

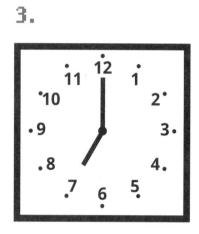

____ : ____

4.

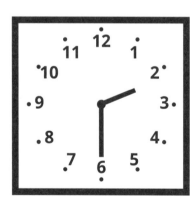

____ : ____

5.

____ : ____

6.

____ : ____

TELLING TIME

Look at the time. Draw the hands on the clock.

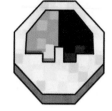

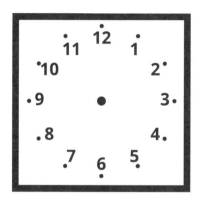

1:00

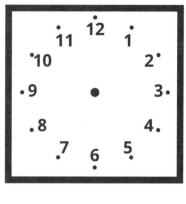

4:00

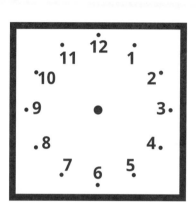

11:30

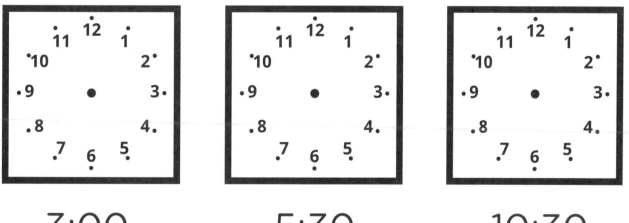

3:00

5:30

10:30

FRACTIONS

Write a fraction to tell about the shaded area. The first one is done for you.

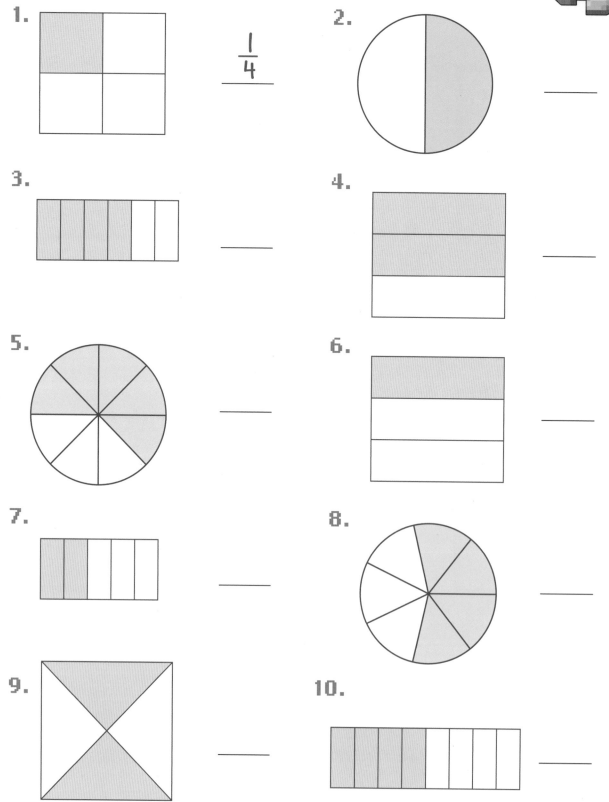

1.

$\dfrac{1}{4}$

2.

_____

3.

_____

4.

_____

5.

_____

6.

_____

7.

_____

8.

_____

9.

_____

10.

_____

126

FRACTIONS

Color each shape to match the fraction.
The first one is done for you.

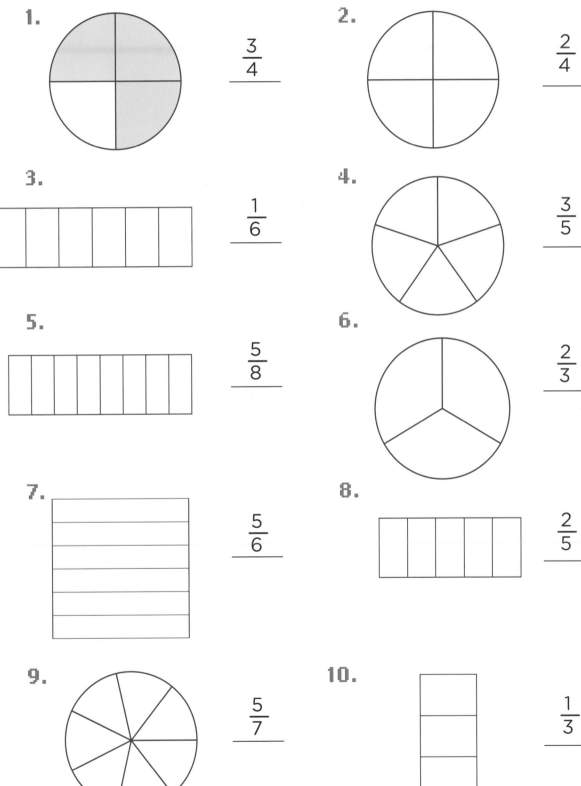

1.

$\dfrac{3}{4}$

2.

$\dfrac{2}{4}$

3.

$\dfrac{1}{6}$

4.

$\dfrac{3}{5}$

5.

$\dfrac{5}{8}$

6.

$\dfrac{2}{3}$

7.

$\dfrac{5}{6}$

8.

$\dfrac{2}{5}$

9.

$\dfrac{5}{7}$

10.

$\dfrac{1}{3}$

FINDING PERIMETER

Perimeter is the distance around a figure.

Find the perimeter of each figure. Each side of a square = 1 cm. The first one is done for you.

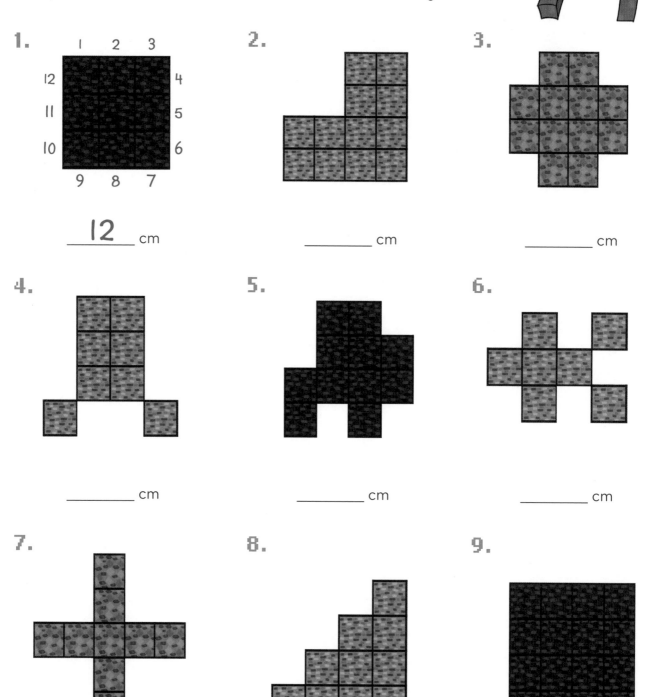

1.

```
   1   2   3
12             4
11             5
10             6
   9   8   7
```

_____12_____ cm

2.

_____ cm

3.

_____ cm

4.

_____ cm

5.

_____ cm

6.

_____ cm

7.

_____ cm

8.

_____ cm

9.

_____ cm

FINDING AREA

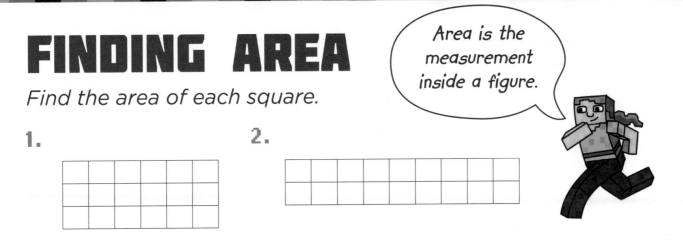

Find the area of each square.

Area is the measurement inside a figure.

1.

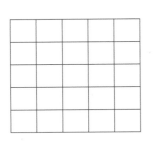

_____ cm

2.

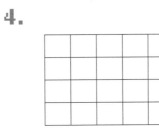

_____ cm

3.

_____ cm

4.

_____ cm

5.

_____ cm

6.

_____ cm

7.

_____ cm

8.

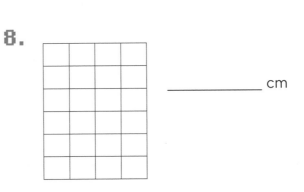

_____ cm

MINECRAFT CONVERTER 1

Use your place value skills to help Enderman convert each of these numbers two different ways. The first one is done for you.

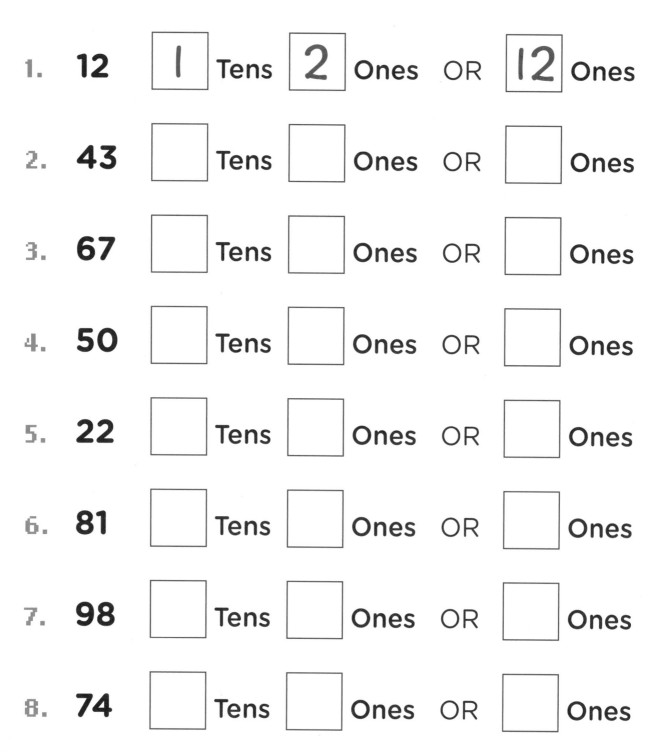

1. **12** | 1 | Tens | 2 | Ones OR | 12 | Ones

2. **43** | | Tens | | Ones OR | | Ones

3. **67** | | Tens | | Ones OR | | Ones

4. **50** | | Tens | | Ones OR | | Ones

5. **22** | | Tens | | Ones OR | | Ones

6. **81** | | Tens | | Ones OR | | Ones

7. **98** | | Tens | | Ones OR | | Ones

8. **74** | | Tens | | Ones OR | | Ones

MINECRAFT CONVERTER 2

Now use your place value skills to help Enderman convert each of these numbers three different ways. The first one is done for you.

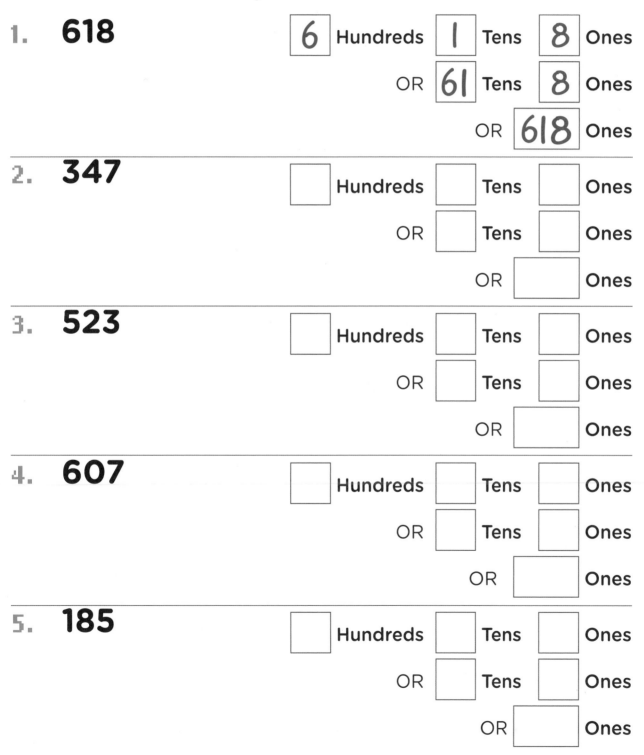

1. **618**   6 Hundreds   1 Tens   8 Ones

        OR   61 Tens   8 Ones

        OR   618 Ones

2. **347**   ☐ Hundreds   ☐ Tens   ☐ Ones

        OR   ☐ Tens   ☐ Ones

        OR   ☐ Ones

3. **523**   ☐ Hundreds   ☐ Tens   ☐ Ones

        OR   ☐ Tens   ☐ Ones

        OR   ☐ Ones

4. **607**   ☐ Hundreds   ☐ Tens   ☐ Ones

        OR   ☐ Tens   ☐ Ones

        OR   ☐ Ones

5. **185**   ☐ Hundreds   ☐ Tens   ☐ Ones

        OR   ☐ Tens   ☐ Ones

        OR   ☐ Ones

NUMBERS BETWEEN

Write the number that goes between.

1. **3,578** ☐ ☐ ☐ ☐ **3,580**

2. **4,090** ☐ ☐ ☐ ☐ **4,092**

3. **2,999** ☐ ☐ ☐ ☐ **3,001**

4. **7,777** ☐ ☐ ☐ ☐ **7,779**

5. **6,002** ☐ ☐ ☐ ☐ **6,004**

6. **1,363** ☐ ☐ ☐ ☐ **1,365**

7. **5,890** ☐ ☐ ☐ ☐ **5,892**

8. **8,000** ☐ ☐ ☐ ☐ **8,002**

EXPLODING NUMBERS

Use place value to write the numbers that Creeper exploded.

1. **3,548** = 3,000 + 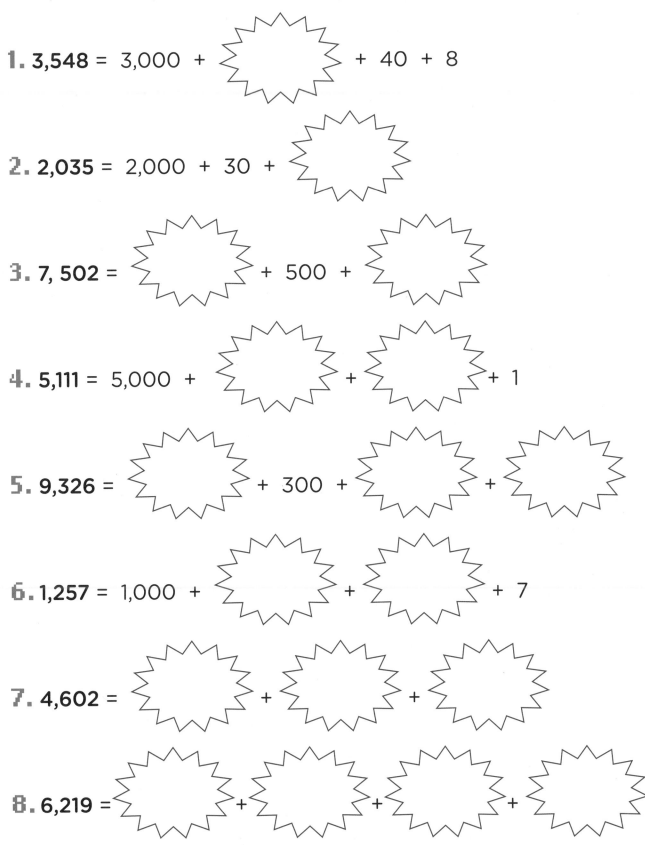 + 40 + 8

2. **2,035** = 2,000 + 30 +

3. **7, 502** =   + 500 +

4. **5,111** = 5,000 +   +   + 1

5. **9,326** =   + 300 +   +

6. **1,257** = 1,000 +   +   + 7

7. **4,602** =   +   +

8. **6,219** =   +   +   +

ADD TO 100

Draw each problem using lines for tens and dots for ones. Then count and add. The first one is done for you.

$| = 10$ $\bullet = 1$

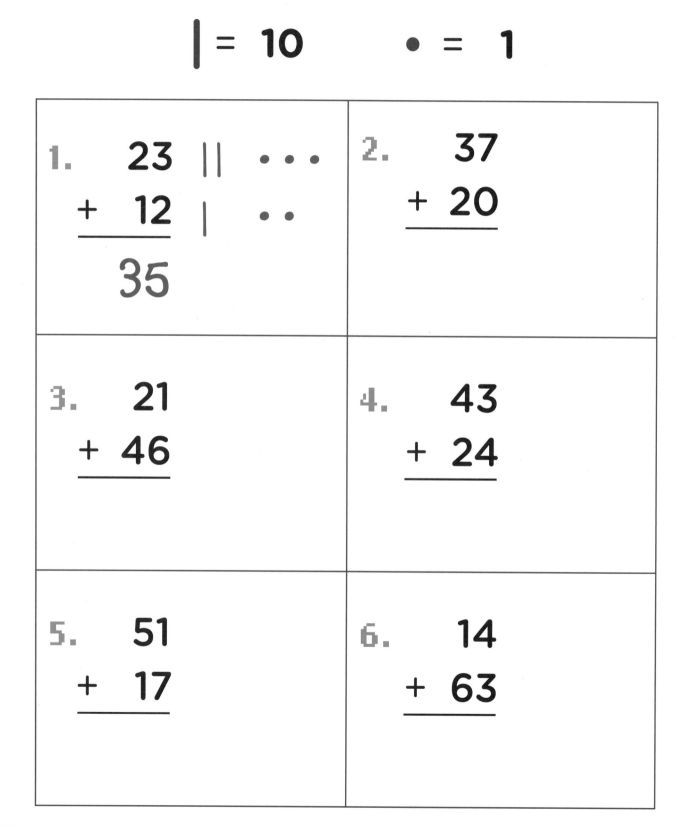

1. 23 || • • •
    + 12 | • •
    ___
    35

2. 37
    + 20
    ___

3. 21
    + 46
    ___

4. 43
    + 24
    ___

5. 51
    + 17
    ___

6. 14
    + 63
    ___

ADD TO 100

Solve each problem. Use the answers to solve the riddle.

1. 15 + 13 **D**	2. 26 + 51 **A**	3. 64 + 12 **O**
4. 21 + 36 **N**	5. 77 + 11 **R**	6. 42 + 52 **M**
7. 33 + 41 **I**	8. 45 + 22 **E**	9. 50 + 23 **S**

Q: *What might Steve mine for in a deck of cards?*

A: __ __ __   __ __ __ __ __ __ __ __

88   67   28   28   74   77   94   76   57   28   73

SUBTRACT WITHIN 100

Draw each top number using lines for tens and dots for ones.
Then subtract the lines and dots for the second number.
Write the number that's left. The first one is done for you.

$$| = 10 \qquad \bullet = 1$$

1.　　33　$|\ |\ \cancel{|}\ \bullet\ \bullet\ \cancel{\bullet}$
　　　− 11
　　　‾‾‾‾‾
　　　22

2.　　56
　　　− 32
　　　‾‾‾‾‾

3.　　45
　　　− 22
　　　‾‾‾‾‾

4.　　85
　　　− 61
　　　‾‾‾‾‾

5.　　72
　　　− 41
　　　‾‾‾‾‾

6.　　68
　　　− 31
　　　‾‾‾‾‾

SUBTRACT WITHIN 100

Solve each problem. Use the answer to solve the riddle.

1. $85 - 33$ **H**	2. $51 - 21$ **M**	3. $66 - 45$ **O**
4. $72 - 30$ **S**	5. $47 - 16$ **R**	6. $49 - 24$ **U**
7. $63 - 33$ **M**	8. $36 - 12$ **A**	9. $64 - 43$ **O**

Q: *What kind of room has no windows and no doors and can be found in dark places throughout the Minecraft world?*

A: __ __ __ __ __ __ __ __ __

24   30 25 42 52 31 21 21 30

ADDITION AND SUBTRACTION

Add or subtract to solve the problems. Watch the signs! Then use the answer to solve the riddle.

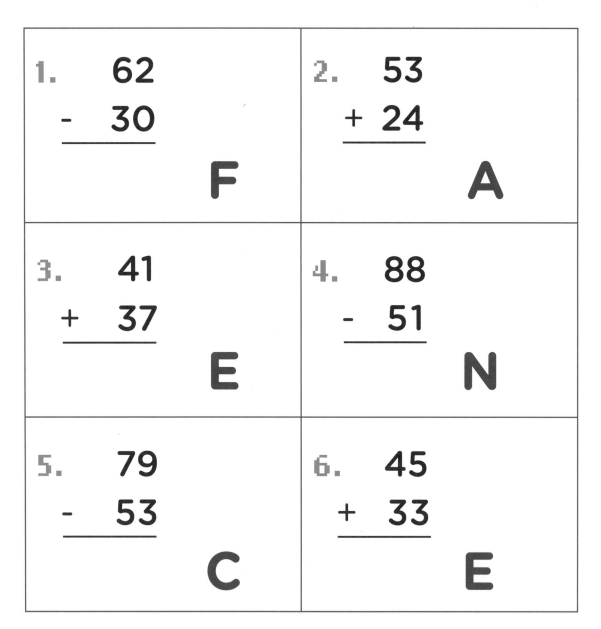

1.
   $$\begin{array}{r} 62 \\ -\ 30 \\ \hline \end{array}$$
   F

2.
   $$\begin{array}{r} 53 \\ +\ 24 \\ \hline \end{array}$$
   A

3.
   $$\begin{array}{r} 41 \\ +\ 37 \\ \hline \end{array}$$
   E

4.
   $$\begin{array}{r} 88 \\ -\ 51 \\ \hline \end{array}$$
   N

5.
   $$\begin{array}{r} 79 \\ -\ 53 \\ \hline \end{array}$$
   C

6.
   $$\begin{array}{r} 45 \\ +\ 33 \\ \hline \end{array}$$
   E

Q: *What runs around Alex's farm without moving?*

A: __ __ __ __ __ __
77   32 78 37 26 78

MIX-UP ON THE FARM

Add or subtract to solve the problems on the farm.

1. The animals on Alex's farm are all mixed up. There are 7 horses in the pig pen, 13 pigs in the pond, 4 ducks in the stables, 9 chickens in the milking barn, and 5 cows in the henhouse. How many animals are on Alex's farm altogether?

   _____

2. Alex moves the 13 pigs out of the pond and to the pigpen. But when she counts the pigs, she only has 6. How many pigs did she lose on the way to the pigpen?

   _____

3. Alex moves 7 horses, 4 ducks, and 5 cows at the same time. How many animals did Alex move at the same time?

   _____

4. Alex has 38 animals on her farm. She wants to have 59 animals. How many more animals does Alex need?

   _____

Which animals do you think Alex should add to her farm?

A. _____

B. _____

BLOCK SQUARES

Count the squares to find them all.

Hint: There's more than 30!

There are _____ squares.

BLOCK PUZZLE

Add and subtract to complete the puzzle.

8	+	7	=	1	5
+					+
3 0	+	3 2	=		2
-				=	
1	2	+		=	1 9
+		2		1	
8	+		=		
=		=			
	+	5	-		=	2
	5				

TREE MATH

Complete each tree. Each number is the total of the two numbers below it. The first one is done for you.

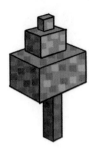

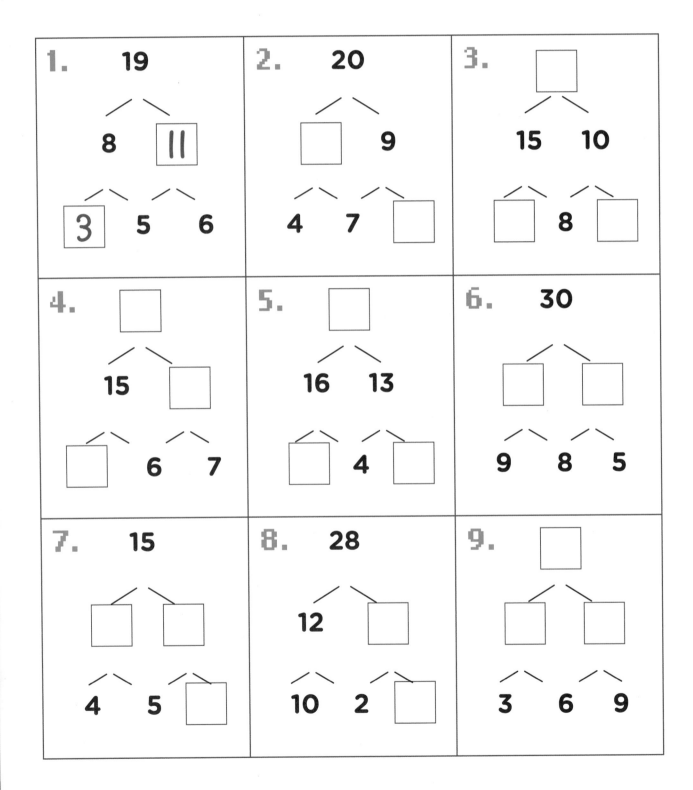

1. 19

8 |11|

[3]   5   6

2. 20

[ ]   9

4   7   [ ]

3. [ ]

15   10

[ ]   8   [ ]

4. [ ]

15   [ ]

[ ]   6   7

5. [ ]

16   13

[ ]   4   [ ]

6. 30

[ ]   [ ]

9   8   5

7. 15

[ ]   [ ]

4   5   [ ]

8. 28

12   [ ]

10   2   [ ]

9. [ ]

[ ]   [ ]

3   6   9

BEEHIVE MATH

Complete the beehive. Each number is the total of the two numbers below it. The first one is done for you. Create your own problem to solve in the last one.

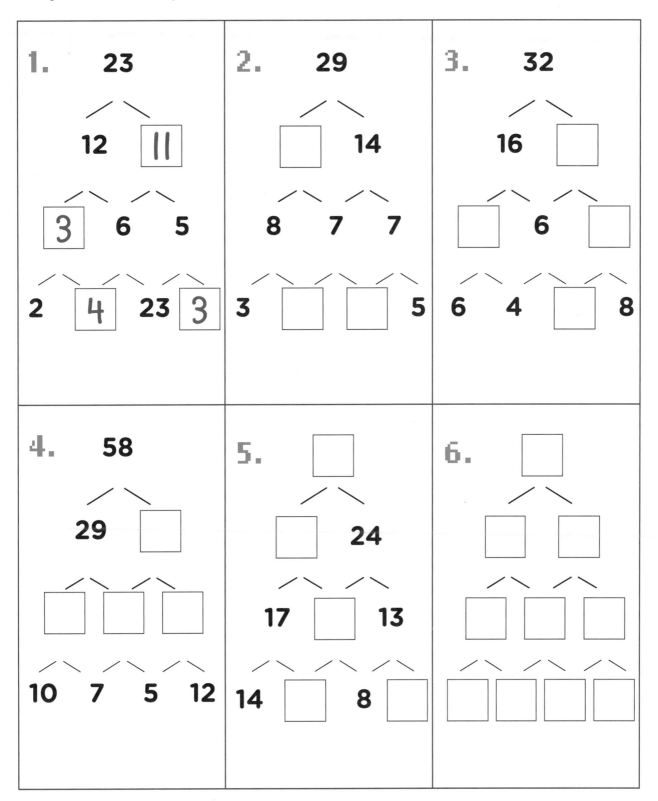

1. 23
12 |1|
3   6   5
2   4   23   3

2. 29
☐   14
8   7   7
3   ☐   ☐   5

3. 32
16   ☐
☐   6   ☐
6   4   ☐   8

4. 58
29   ☐
☐   ☐   ☐
10   7   5   12

5. ☐
☐   24
17   ☐   13
14   ☐   8   ☐

6. ☐
☐   ☐
☐   ☐   ☐
☐   ☐   ☐   ☐

MATH LOGIC

Use your logic to solve these problems.

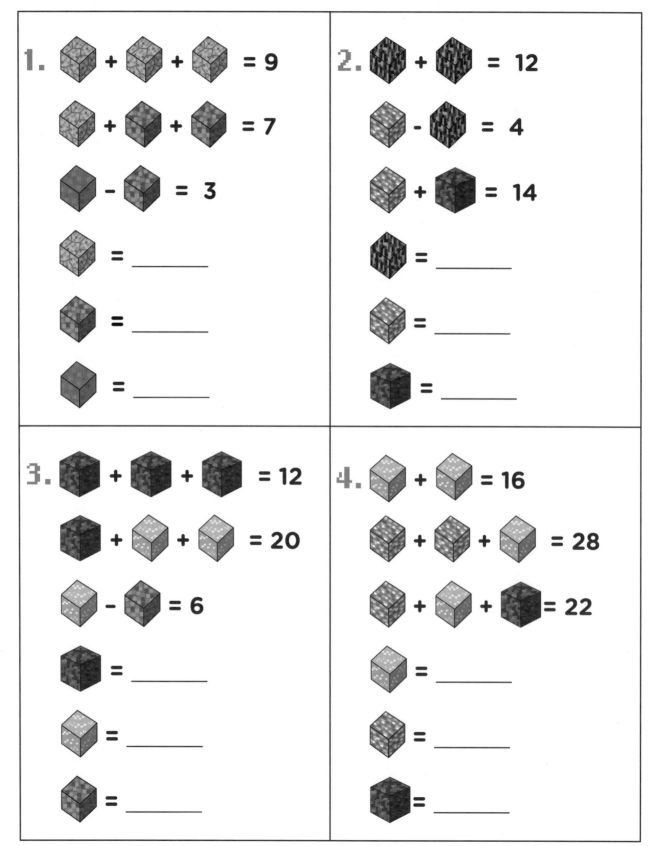

1. ▢ + ▢ + ▢ = 9

▢ + ▢ + ▢ = 7

▢ – ▢ = 3

▢ = _____

▢ = _____

▢ = _____

2. ▢ + ▢ = 12

▢ – ▢ = 4

▢ + ▢ = 14

▢ = _____

▢ = _____

▢ = _____

3. ▢ + ▢ + ▢ = 12

▢ + ▢ + ▢ = 20

▢ – ▢ = 6

▢ = _____

▢ = _____

▢ = _____

4. ▢ + ▢ = 16

▢ + ▢ + ▢ = 28

▢ + ▢ + ▢ = 22

▢ = _____

▢ = _____

▢ = _____

READING FOR MINECRAFTERS

RHYMING WORDS

Draw a line to connect the rhyming words.

1. cat

2. egg

3. clock

4. porch

5. head

A.

B.

C.

D.

E.

LONG OR SHORT VOWEL SOUND

Say each word. Listen for the vowel sound.
Circle long or short.

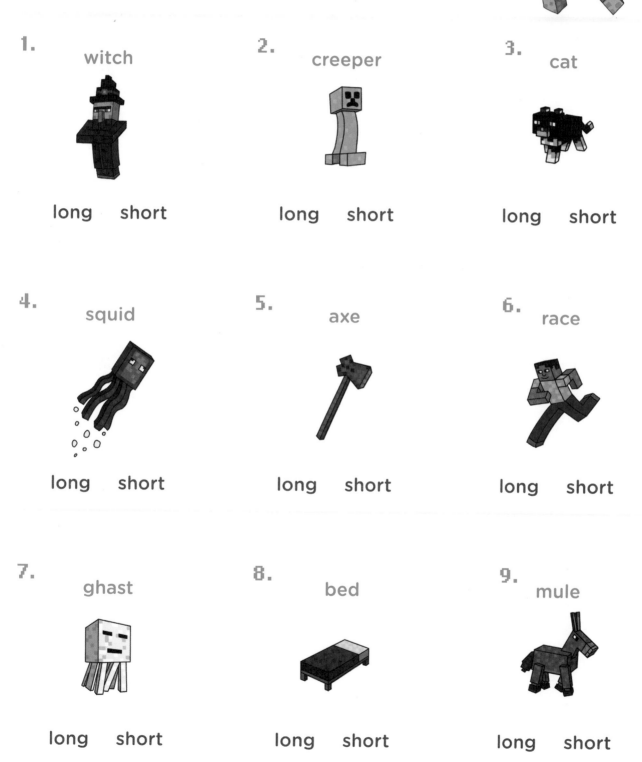

1. witch

    long   short

2. creeper

    long   short

3. cat

    long   short

4. squid

    long   short

5. axe

    long   short

6. race

    long   short

7. ghast

    long   short

8. bed

    long   short

9. mule

    long   short

SHORT VOWELS

Draw a line to connect the word with the short vowel sound to the matching picture.

1. pig

2. cat

3. bed

4. ocelot

5. sun

A.

B.

C.

D.

E.

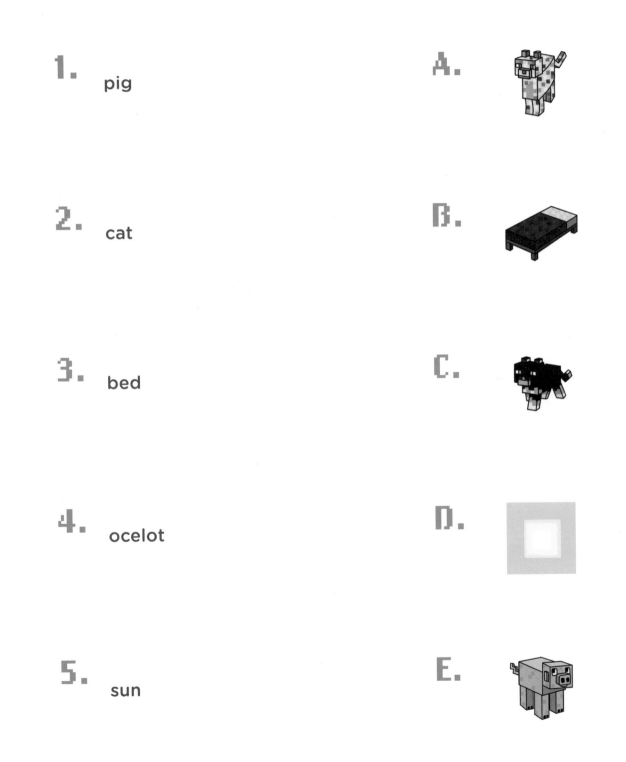

SHORT VOWELS

Circle the word with the short vowel sound that matches each picture.

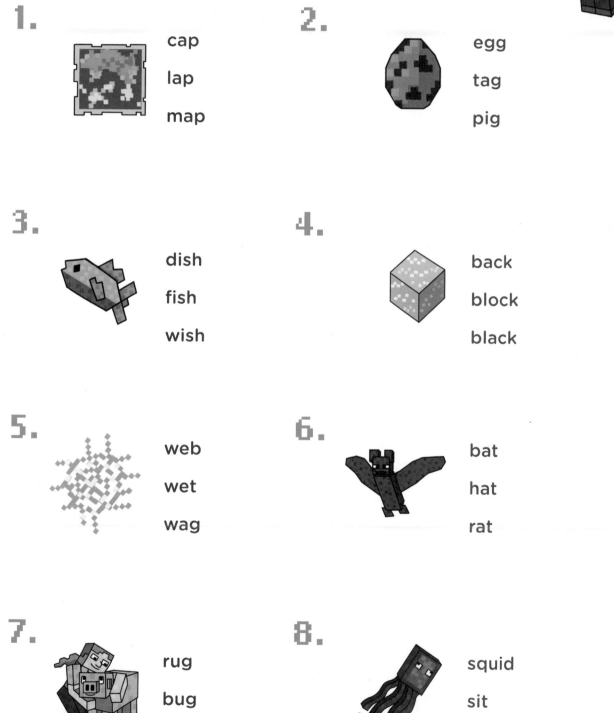

1.
cap
lap
map

2.
egg
tag
pig

3.
dish
fish
wish

4.
back
block
black

5.
web
wet
wag

6.
bat
hat
rat

7.
rug
bug
hug

8.
squid
sit
sad

LONG VOWELS

The silent *e* at the end of the word makes the vowel long.

All the words below have long vowel sounds. Write the missing vowel in each word.

1.  c __ k e

2.  b __ n e

3.  m __ l e

4.  r __ d e

5.  c __ b e

LONG VOWELS

When two vowels are together in a word, the first is long and the second is silent.

The first vowel in each word below is long. Draw a line to connect the word to the matching picture.

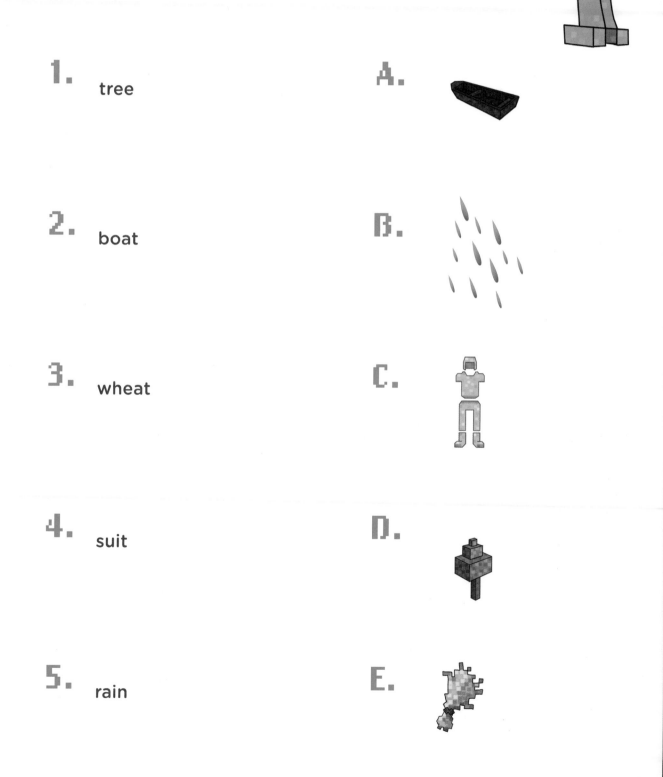

1. tree

2. boat

3. wheat

4. suit

5. rain

A.

B.

C.

D.

E.

LONG AND SHORT VOWELS

*Fill in the missing vowel team to complete the word. Circle **long** or **short** to describe the sound the vowel makes.*

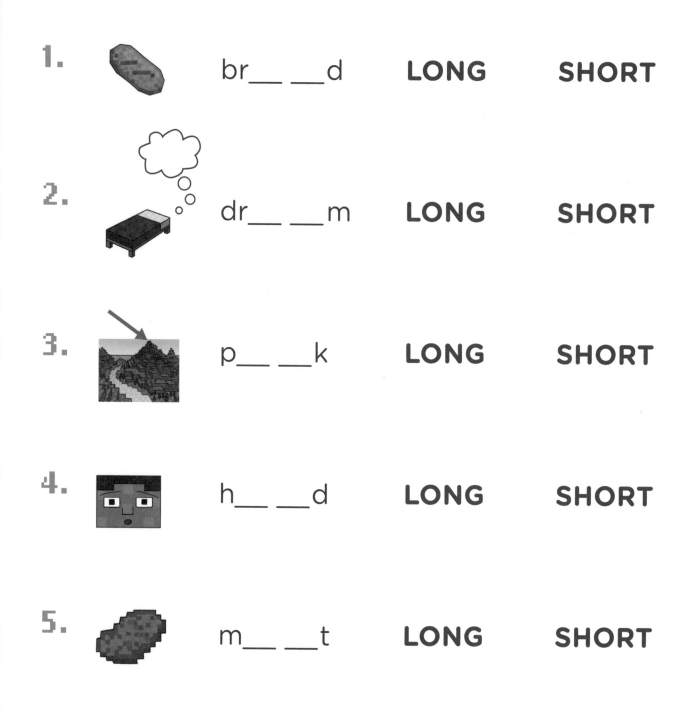

1. br__ __d   **LONG**   **SHORT**

2. dr__ __m   **LONG**   **SHORT**

3. p__ __k   **LONG**   **SHORT**

4. h__ __d   **LONG**   **SHORT**

5. m__ __t   **LONG**   **SHORT**

WORD FILL-IN

*Use the box of **ea** words to finish the sentences below. Circle long or short to describe the sound the vowel makes.*

| beat | Beach | team | dead | seat |

1. You will find sand in a _____ Biome. **LONG** **SHORT**

2. If you get tired of walking, you can make a _____ _____. **LONG** **SHORT**

3. Join with other players as a _____ . **LONG** **SHORT**

4. Zombies are easy to _____ with sunlight. **LONG** **SHORT**

5. When you have no health points left, you are _____ _____ . **LONG** **SHORT**

MISSING LETTERS

*What letters are missing from the **bossy r (r-controlled)** words below? Choose **ar, er, ir, or,** or **ur**. Write the full word on the line with the added letters underlined.*

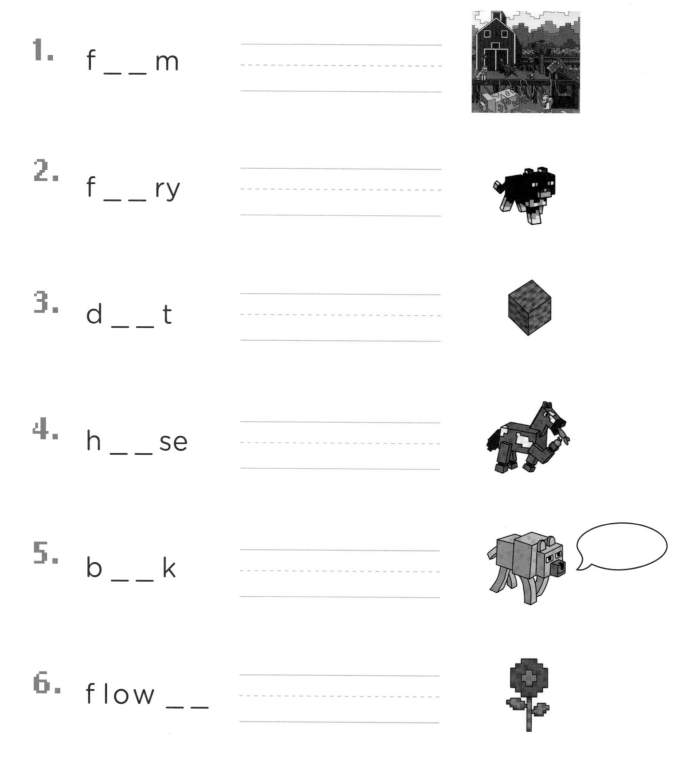

1. f _ _ m

2. f _ _ ry

3. d _ _ t

4. h _ _ se

5. b _ _ k

6. f l o w _ _

WORD FILL-IN

*Use the box of **bossy r (r-controlled)** words to finish the sentences below.*

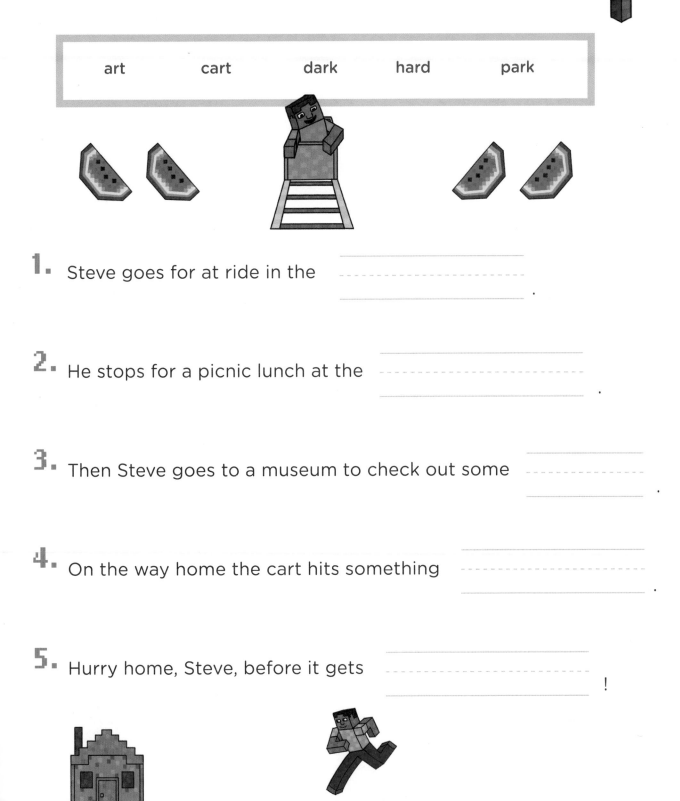

art	cart	dark	hard	park

1. Steve goes for at ride in the _____ .

2. He stops for a picnic lunch at the _____ .

3. Then Steve goes to a museum to check out some _____ .

4. On the way home the cart hits something _____ .

5. Hurry home, Steve, before it gets _____ !

WORD FILL-IN

*Use the box of **-ight** words to finish the sentences below.*

right	might	sight	flight	bright

1. The bat took _____ .

2. It flew _____ into lava.

3. It was quite a _____ to see!

4. You never know what you _____ discover in Minecraft.

5. Keep your _____ eyes open.

STEVE'S WORD SCRAMBLE

*Unscramble the **-ight** words below. Write them correctly on the line.*

1. ghnit

2. tshig

3. irgbht

4. hftgi

5. lhigtf

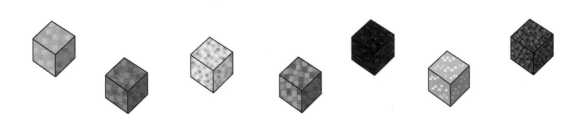

WITHER'S WORD SEARCH

Can you find and circle all the words from the list?

blast	body	build	camp
chest	craft	fast	food
jump	mind	read	sand
size	test	went	wind

P Y D O B T S A F J

M L T T P D S O T T

U D F B A M O A N D

J D A E T D A E L Z

R M R M T S W C M B

T L C E T B I I J T

L P S M S M U Z N L

B T I L E A D I E D

D N D L H T N R L N

D P W Q C V L D V D

WITHER'S WORD SEARCH

Can you find and circle all the words from the list?

art	bark	cart	dark
farm	flower	furry	hard
horse	know	little	new
only	park	place	take
			dirt

T R I D E R K E B W
R E Y H E L C R N X
A Y K W O A T D A N
C D O A L R K T D B
B L M P T R S R I X
F U R R Y D O E A L
K D R A H A M N N P
N T M Y N R B E L X
O R R W A K W M T Y
W A J F N X N B T K

ENDING BLENDS

What letters are missing from the words below? Write the full word on the line with the added letters underlined. Use the word bank below to help.

chest	blast	sand	craft	fast

1. bla _ _

2. sa _ _

3. fa _ _

4. che _ _

5. cra _ _

WORD FILL-IN

*Use the box of words with **ending blends** to finish the sentences below.*

camp	test	jump	mind	wind

1. Donkeys can't _____ as high as horses.

2. Survival maps _____ your fighting and survival skills.

3. We built a great _____ site with a fire pit.

4. If a villager stops accepting a trade, trade other items until he changes his _____ .

5. You can make waves and _____ with mods.

ENDING BLENDS

What letters are missing from the words below? Write the full word on the line with the added letters underlined. Use the word bank below to help.

clock	church	block	torch	bush

1. blo _ _

2. clo _ _

3. tor _ _

4. bu _ _

5. chur _ _

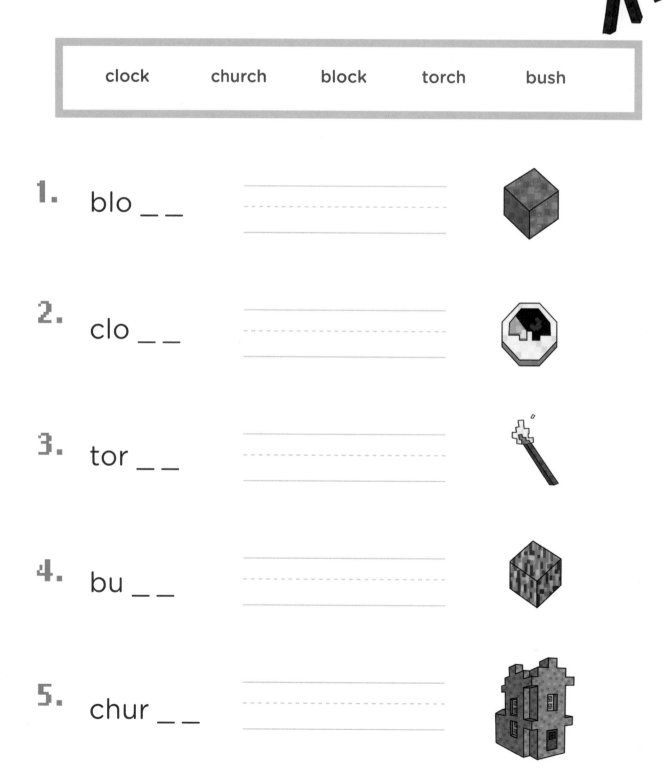

WORD FILL-IN

Use the box of words with **ending blends** to finish the sentences below.

much	wish	search	rich	rush

1. It is _____ easier to beat the Wither with the help of friends.

2. He is _____ in iron, gold, and diamonds.

3. What do you _____ for in new Minecraft releases?

4. It is fun to explore and _____ for new biomes.

5. To fight blazes, use Fire Resistance potions and _____ them as they start to rise in the air.

MISSING LETTERS

*What **letter team** is missing from all of the words below? Write the full word on the line with the added letters underlined.*

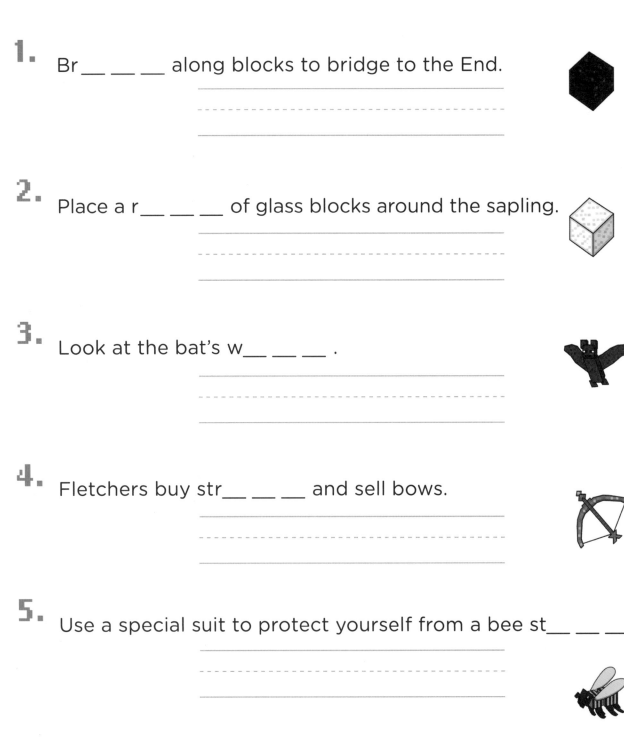

1. Br __ __ __ along blocks to bridge to the End.

2. Place a r __ __ __ of glass blocks around the sapling.

3. Look at the bat's w __ __ __ .

4. Fletchers buy str __ __ __ and sell bows.

5. Use a special suit to protect yourself from a bee st __ __ __ .

STEVE'S WORD SCRAMBLE

*Unscramble the **-ing** words below. Write them correctly on the line.*

1. gisn

2. gnki

3. lsgin

4. gicln

5. prgsni

READING WORDS

Read each word. Draw a line to match the word to the picture.

1. beacon

A.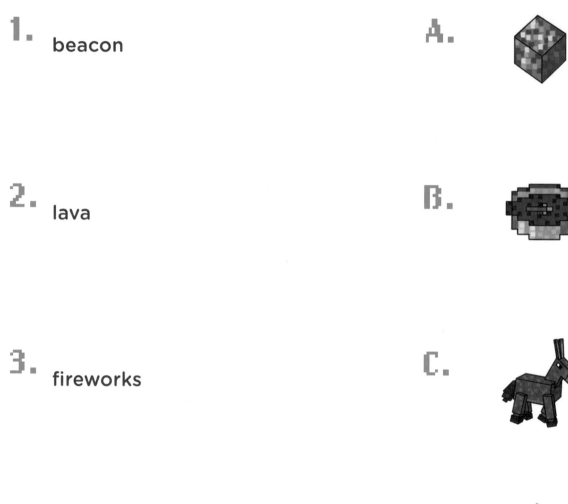

2. lava

B.

3. fireworks

C.

4. donkey

D.

5. compass

E.

READING WORDS

Circle the word that matches each picture.

1.

chest

chess

cheat

2.

sears

cheers

shears

3.

shell

shield

shed

4.

thed

threat

thread

5.

wet

wheat

what

6.

house

hows

hoss

7.

torsh

troch

torch

8.

bred

bread

bed

WHAT DO YOU KNOW?

Look at the characters below. Finish the sentence about each Minecrafting character or mob using what you see or know. The first one is done for you.

1. Alex has _____ a carrot _____.

2. The bee is _____ .

3. The camel has _____ .

4. The chicken is _____ .

5. The armor is _____ .

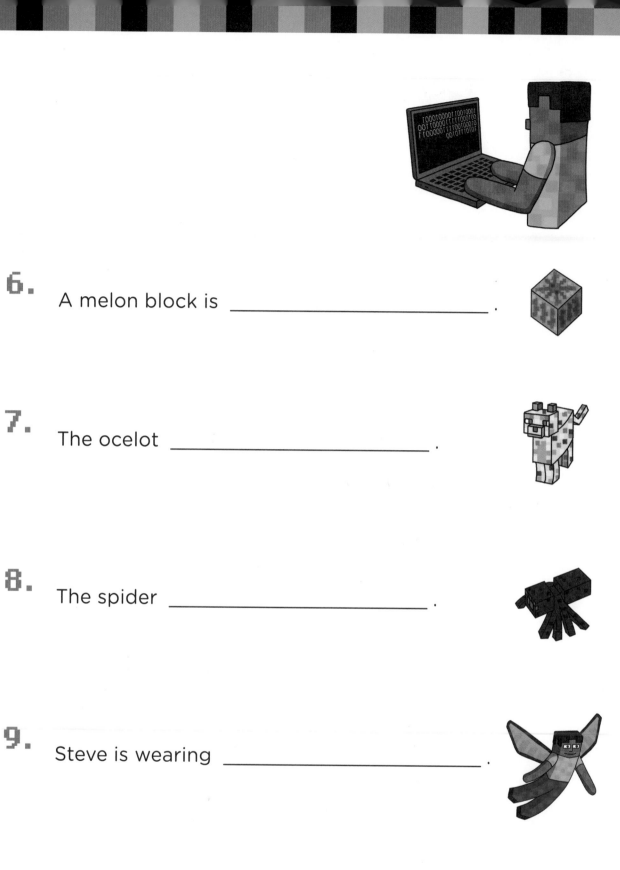

6. A melon block is _____ .

7. The ocelot _____ .

8. The spider _____ .

9. Steve is wearing _____ .

10. Witches can _____ .

WHAT DOES IT MEAN?

*Read each sentence. Use the context to figure out the meaning of the **bolded** word. Then circle the best meaning.*

1.

The **hostile** mobs are not friendly.

> **HOSTILE** means:
>
> nice   ***or***   mean

2.

The **residents** live in the city.

> **RESIDENTS** are:
>
> people who live in a place   ***or***   monsters who destroy

3.

The mobs **spawn** baby mobs.

> **SPAWN** means:
>
> to destroy   ***or***   to create

4.

The Minecraft **biomes** include Jungle, Ice Plains, Forest, and the End.

> **BIOMES** are:
>
> mobs   ***or***   places

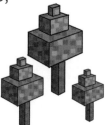

WHAT DOES IT MEAN?

*Read each sentence. Use the context to figure out the meaning of the **bolded** word. Then circle the best meaning.*

1. The **neutral** mobs will not help or hurt you.

> **NEUTRAL** means:
>
> neither bad nor good   **or**   angry and attacking

2. Sheep and rabbits live in the large trees of the **taiga**.

> **TAIGA** means:
>
> a hot desert   **or**   a swampy forest

3. The **void** is pure black and empty.

> **VOID** means:
>
> nothing there   **or**   full of life

4. The creeper's explosions make it a **destructive** mob.

> **DESTRUCTIVE** means:
>
> friendly   **or**   dangerous

OPPOSITES

Draw a line to each opposite.

1.  sit

A. night

2.  little

B.  hostile

3. day

C.  big

4.  friendly

D. stand

MORE OPPOSITES

Write the correct choice of opposites to complete each sentence.

1. Iron golem _____ villager a flower.

   gives / takes

2. The chest is _____ .

   open / closed

3. Creeper is _____ the trap.

   inside / outside

4. Squid is swimming _____ .

   up / down

POSITION WORDS

Complete each sentence with the correct word. Some words may be used more than once.

in	beside	in front of	on	behind

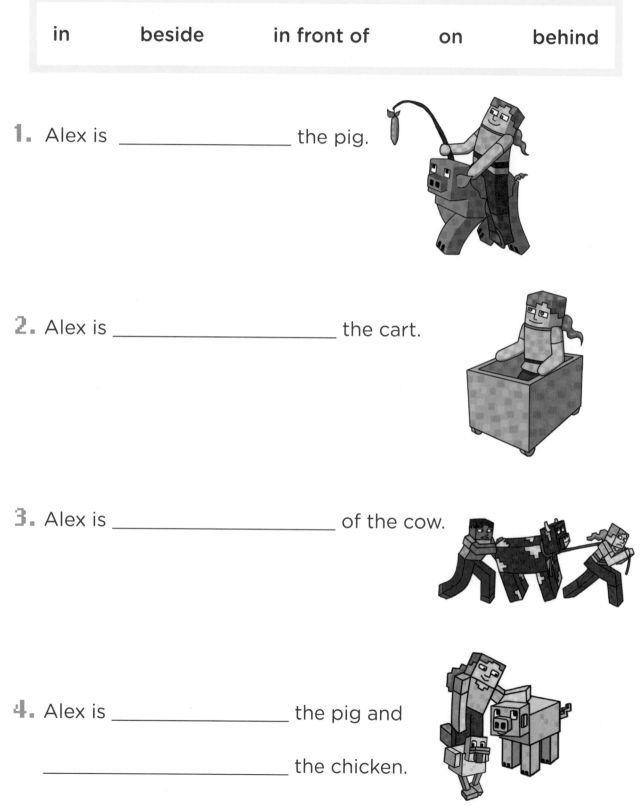

1. Alex is _____ the pig.

2. Alex is _____ the cart.

3. Alex is _____ of the cow.

4. Alex is _____ the pig and

_____ the chicken.

POSITION WORDS

Look at the picture. Circle the word that best completes each sentence.

1. Ocelot is **by   behind**   the river.

2. Monkey sits **on   under** the tree.

3. The clouds float **under   in** the sky.

4. Parrot flies **below   above** the river.

5. The trees grow **inside   beside** the river.

WORDS AND PICTURES

Read or listen to this informational text about the city. Look at the picture. Then answer the questions on the next page.

THE CITY

A very experienced gamer built this block city. It is made of blocks of clay and glass.

The city has tall buildings. There is a church, a school, shops, and many houses.

Some villagers live in the city. They have many jobs. Visiting villagers come to the city for a vacation. There are many ways to get around the city. Villagers can walk, ride the train, or take a boat.

Answer the questions about the city. Circle W if you get the answer from the words. Circle P if you get the answer from the picture. Circle both if you used both the words and picture to answer the question.

1. What is the city near? W P

2. What is the city made of? W P

3. What does the city look like? W P

4. Who is in the city? W P

5. How can villagers get around the city? W P

REMEMBERING DETAILS

Steve is exploring the shipwreck site. Study the picture for a minute or two. When you think you have memorized the details, cover the picture and try to answer the questions on the next page.

REMEMBERING DETAILS (continued from previous page)

Answer the questions in the space provided.

1. Name one animal in the scene besides a fish.

_____.

2. How many masts does the ship have?

_____.

3. What color are Steve's flippers?

_____.

4. What is the largest animal in the scene?

_____.

5. Which animal is in the lower right corner?

_____.

STRUCTURE OF A STORY

Read or listen to the story. Draw pictures to tell the story.

STEVE MEETS A ZOMBIE

It is late. The sun has already gone down. Steve walks through the woods.

Suddenly, a zombie attacks! They battle. Steve shoots his bow and arrow. The zombie hits back hard. Steve shoots another arrow, but the zombie fights back. Steve shoots one final arrow.

Zing! Steve destroys the zombie.

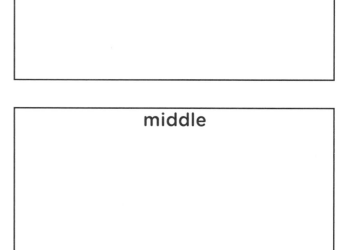

beginning

middle

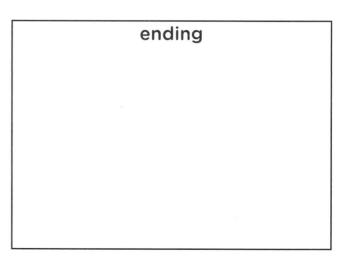

ending

STRUCTURE OF A STORY

Read or listen to the story. Draw pictures to tell the story.

beginning

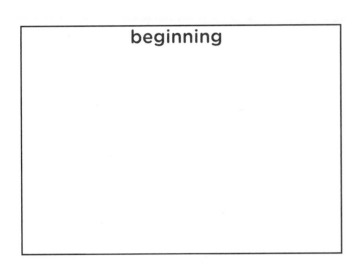

middle

ending

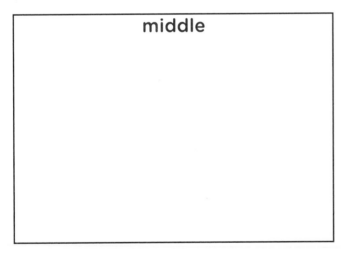

SKELETON ATTACK!

"The skeletons are coming," Steve shouted. A group of skeletons followed right behind Steve as he ran back to his farm to protect it. His loyal dog was right beside him.

Steve turned around and drew his golden sword. He struck one skeleton while his dog leaped up to bite the other skeletons. The skeletons were no match for this team. Two of the bony beasts were destroyed. The rest ran away.

Steve gathered the bones and arrows with a big smile. The farm was saved!

SEQUENCE EVENTS

Read the passage. Then number the steps (1, 2, 3, 4) to show how to mine for diamonds.

Mining Diamonds

It's easy and fun to mine for diamonds. First, you need to locate a block of diamond ore. Ore is rock that has diamonds in it. Then, chop the diamond ore with an iron pickaxe. When a diamond drops, place it in a chest for safe keeping. Then you can use it to make a diamond sword!

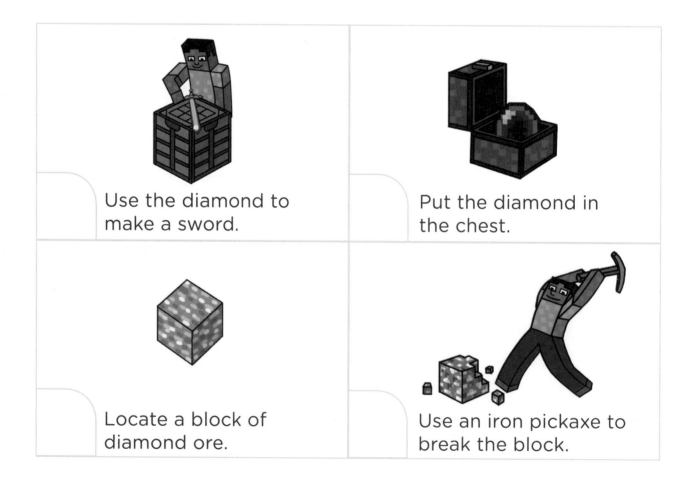

Use the diamond to make a sword.

Put the diamond in the chest.

Locate a block of diamond ore.

Use an iron pickaxe to break the block.

SEQUENCE EVENTS

*Read the passage. Then number the pictures
(1, 2, 3, 4) to show how to ride a pig.*

How to Ride a Pig

If you're an advanced Minecrafter, you can learn to ride a pig!
First, get all the things you need. You need a pig, a saddle, a
carrot, and a stick. Next, put the saddle on the pig's back. Then,
hook the carrot onto the end of the stick and hold it in front of
the pig. Now jump on the pig and enjoy the ride!

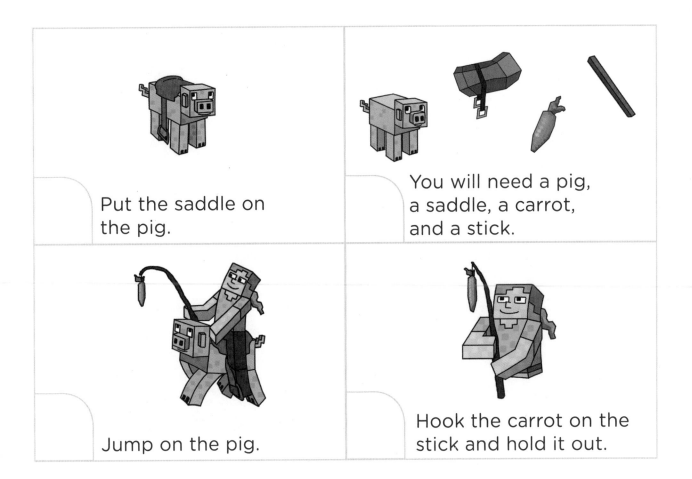

Put the saddle on
the pig.

You will need a pig,
a saddle, a carrot,
and a stick.

Jump on the pig.

Hook the carrot on the
stick and hold it out.

NOUNS

Find and circle the nouns listed at the bottom of the page.

A noun is a person, place, or thing.

yo-yo	book	lamp	shoe
bear	doll	pillow	sock
bed	duck	plant	truck

PLURALS

Write the plural.

Plural means more than one. Most nouns are made plural by adding *s*.

To make the plural of words that end in *o, s, x, ch, sh,* or *th,* add *es*.

Example: *one boss   two boss**es***

1. pig _____

2. potato _____

3. witch _____

4. cow _____

5. bush _____

VERBS

Write the verb that matches the picture.

Verbs are action words. "Hang" is a verb.

run	fight	swim	eat	fly
think	ride	laugh	sit	

1.

2.

3.

4.

5.

6.

7.

8.

9.

PAST TENSE

Draw a line from the present tense verb to its irregular past tense form.

Past tense shows something already happened.

Most verbs show past tense by adding *ed*. Not these words!

1. run

2. fight

3. eat

4. ride

5. think

A. rode

B. fought

C. thought

D. ran

E. ate

ADJECTIVES ON THE FARM

Choose an adjective to finish each sentence.
Then underline the word that the adjective describes.

spotted	red	white	noisy	hungry	furry	beautiful

1. The farm mobs lived in the _____ barn.

2. The _____ cow mooed loudly.

3. The _____ cat sat on the fence.

4. The _____ horse wanted some hay.

5. The _____ butterfly floated around the farm.

6. The _____ cat chased the rabbit.

7. The _____ rabbit hopped away.

ADVERBS ON THE FARM

Choose an adverb to finish each sentence.
Then underline the word that the adverb describes.

quickly	slowly	gently	patiently
loudly		aimlessly	sleepily

1. Pig oinked _____.

2. The chickens walked _____ around the farm.

3. Alex petted the pig _____.

4. Rabbit hopped _____ to get away from the cat.

5. The spotted cat sat _____ on the fence.

6. The clouds floated _____ across the sky.

7. The horse waited _____ for the hay.

SILLY FILL-IN

Fill in the word blanks below. Read the story at right and add your words as you go. Did it make you laugh?

| **ADJECTIVE** a describing word, like *scary* | **NOUN** a person, place or thing, like *creeper* | **VERB** an action word, like *run* |

1. _____
VERB

2. _____
VERB ENDING IN "ING"

3. _____
NOUN

4. _____
VERB ENDING IN "ING"

5. _____
NUMBER

6. _____
ADJECTIVE

7. _____
FAMILY MEMBER

8. _____
PLURAL NOUN

9. _____
PART OF THE BODY

10. _____
ADJECTIVE

CREEPER GOES TO A BIRTHDAY PARTY

Alex invited a friendly creeper to Steve's birthday party. When they arrived

at Steve's house, the creeper watched the kids _____ in the
                                                      VERB

backyard. He saw streamers and balloons _____ from the
                                            VERB ENDING IN "ING"

ceiling. A _____ was piled with presents, cupcakes, and
               NOUN

potion of _____.
              VERB ENDING IN "ING"

"Hi, Steve," said Alex. "This is my new creeper friend. Happy birthday!"

"What's a birthday?" asked the creeper.

"You need some party hats," Steve said. He put _____ hats
                                                    NUMBER

on the creeper. The creeper looked _____ .
                                        ADJECTIVE

"I think your table is on fire," the creeper said after Steve's

_____ lit the _____ on the cake. The kids
  FAMILY MEMBER   PLURAL NOUN

started to sing "Happy Birthday." The creeper looked frightened. Steve

handed him a piece of cake on a plate with a fork. The creeper didn't know

what the fork was for, so he used his _____ to eat. It was
                                           PART OF THE BODY

an _____ day!
       ADJECTIVE

HOMONYMS

Circle the homonyms in each sentence.

Homonyms are words that sound the same but are spelled differently and have different meanings.

1. A bee can be busy.

2. Steve acts brave with his axe.

3. I saw an eye of an ender.

4. Alex put flour on the flower.

5. Which witch did you see?

SYNONYMS FOR SAID

Synonyms are words that have similar meanings.

*Rewrite each sentence with a synonym for the word **said**. Choose one of the words in the box or write your own.*

| whispered | screamed | shouted | yelled |

1. Creeper said, "Ssssorry, but you must die!"

_____

2. Steve said, "Look out below!"

_____

3. Alex said to the pig, "You are my favorite mob."

_____

4. "I found a diamond!" said Steve excitedly.

_____

ZOMBIE PROBLEMS

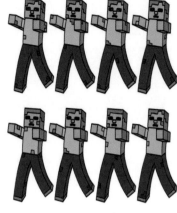

Read the story. Answer the questions.

Early in the morning, a player entered a village. It was still dark. The zombies moaned loudly. The zombies wanted to attack the player. The player heard the zombies. The player ran into a building. But the zombies kept attacking. Nothing could stop the zombies. The player was afraid. The player sat on the floor. Just then, the sun peered through the window. The zombies were gone.

1. Who are the main characters?

_____

_____

_____

2. What was the problem?

_____

_____

_____

3. How was the problem solved?

_____

_____

_____

WITCH PROBLEMS

Read the story. Answer the questions.

One day a villager was struck by lightning. A witch appeared. The player quickly punched the witch. The witch ran from the player and drank some healing potion. The player followed the witch to attack. The witch threw some potion of Slowness at the player. The player slowed down. The witch got away.

1. Who are the main characters?

_____

_____

_____

2. What was the problem?

_____

_____

_____

3. How was the problem solved?

_____

_____

_____

PIG POEM

Read the poem. Circle the correct answers to the questions.

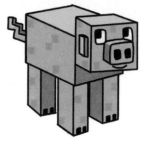

A pig is a passive mob
with only one small job.

A pig's job is to oink all day
and stay far away from clay.

To find a pig no need for glasses.
Just look in places with lots of grasses.

If you have a saddle, you can ride
upon a pig who hasn't died.

For when they die they will drop
a tasty little porkchop.

1. *What is the main idea of the poem?*

    A. to learn to tame a pig

    B. to learn where to find a pig

    C. to learn about pigs in Minecraft

2. *What is the job of a pig?*

    A. to oink all day

    B. to stay away from clay

    C. both A and B

3. *What will a pig drop when it dies?*

    A. its saddle

    B. a porkchop

    C. its glasses

STEVE THE PLAYER

Read about Steve. Circle the correct answer to the questions.

Steve likes to play in Minecraft. He has lots of fun. Steve likes to craft new tools. He likes to mine for iron and ore. He likes to explore new places. Steve is a good sport because he tries his best and has fun.

1. *What is the main idea?*

   A. Steve is the best Minecraft player.

   B. Steve likes to play in Minecraft.

   C. Steve likes to hang upside down.

2. *What does it mean to be a good sport?*

   A. to try your best and have fun

   B. to be good at sports

   C. to play Minecraft a lot

3. *Write about what you like to do in Minecraft.*

_____

_____

_____

_____

_____

ENDERMAN ART

Follow the directions to draw an enderman.
Use a ruler or estimate the measurements.

1. Draw a 2″ x 1″ rectangle at the top of the space.

2. Draw a 2″ x 2″ square below the rectangle. The rectangle and the square should touch.

3. Draw a thin rectangle about ¼″ x 4½″. The thin rectangle should touch the top right of the square.

4. Draw another thin rectangle ¼″ x 4½″ on the other side of the square.

5. Draw another thin rectangle ¼″ x 4½″ below the square. The rectangle should touch the square on the bottom right side of the square.

6. Draw another thin rectangle on the other side of the square.

7. Draw two eyes in the middle of the top rectangle. The eyes should be thin rectangles.

HAVE YOU SEEN MY CHICKEN?

*Read a conversation between Alex and Steve.
Answer the question.*

Alex: Have you seen my chicken?

Steve: Yeah, I have seen your chicken.

Alex: Really? My chicken is white.

Steve: I saw a white chicken.

Alex: My chicken has an orange beak and two orange legs.

Steve: I saw a white chicken with an orange beak and two orange legs.

Alex: My chicken lays eggs.

Steve: I saw a white chicken with an orange beak and two orange legs laying eggs.

Alex: You have seen my chicken! Where is it?

Steve: I don't know. I saw it yesterday.

Did Steve help Alex find her chicken? Explain.

_____

_____

_____

_____

BIRTHDAY PRESENT MIX-UP

Today is Creeper's birthday. Many of the characters from the Minecraft world brought gifts, but some of the presents lost their tags. Use the clues to write the correct names on the tags.

CLUES: Skeleton's present has a bow.

Steve's present has a blue bow. It is bigger than Skeleton's present.

Alex's present is the biggest.

The villager's present doesn't have a blue bow.

1.

From:

2.

From:

3.

From:

4.

From:

CREEPER'S BIRTHDAY

Read the clues. Draw a picture showing what each character gave Creeper for his birthday.

1. Skeleton gave Creeper something he likes to listen to.

2. Steve gave Creeper something to make him impossible to see.

3. Alex gave Creeper his favorite plant.

4. The zombie villagers gave Creeper something to climb.

FOLLOW YOUR OWN MINECRAFT ADVENTURE

Follow the arrows on the chart to find the loot.

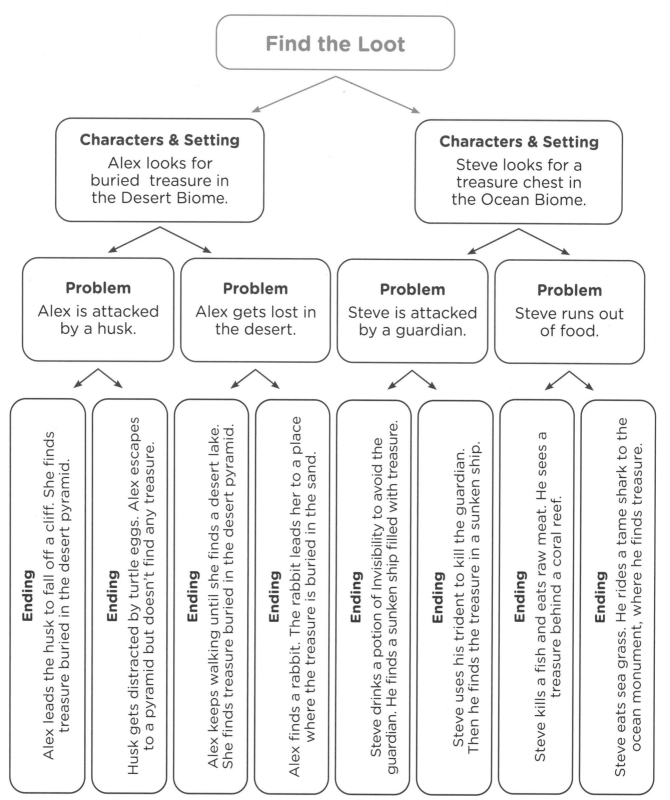

Find the Loot

Characters & Setting
Alex looks for buried treasure in the Desert Biome.

Characters & Setting
Steve looks for a treasure chest in the Ocean Biome.

Problem
Alex is attacked by a husk.

Problem
Alex gets lost in the desert.

Problem
Steve is attacked by a guardian.

Problem
Steve runs out of food.

Ending
Alex leads the husk to fall off a cliff. She finds treasure buried in the desert pyramid.

Ending
Husk gets distracted by turtle eggs. Alex escapes to a pyramid but doesn't find any treasure.

Ending
Alex keeps walking until she finds a desert lake. She finds treasure buried in the desert pyramid.

Ending
Alex finds a rabbit. The rabbit leads her to a place where the treasure is buried in the sand.

Ending
Steve drinks a potion of Invisibility to avoid the guardian. He finds a sunken ship filled with treasure.

Ending
Steve uses his trident to kill the guardian. Then he finds the treasure in a sunken ship.

Ending
Steve kills a fish and eats raw meat. He sees a treasure behind a coral reef.

Ending
Steve eats sea grass. He rides a tame shark to the ocean monument, where he finds treasure.

WRITE YOUR OWN ADVENTURE

Use your choices from page 202 to write your adventure story.

Find the Loot

_____

_____

_____

_____

_____

_____

_____

_____

_____

_____

_____

ANSWER QUESTIONS

Read the story. Answer the questions.

THE LIBRARY

The library is filled with books about building. Mobs come to the library to find a book of enchantment. Today Steve is going to the library. He wants to find a special book to make him more powerful so he can defeat the Wither.

Once inside the library, Steve meets the librarian. The librarian tells him he must climb the stairs and find the trap door. Then he will find the book.

It is dark in the library. Steve must carry a torch. Finally, Steve finds his way to the trap door. He pulls a lever. The door opens. Inside the room, he finds the book he was looking for. He takes the book home and learns how to enchant his weapons. Later that day, he defeats the Wither!

1. Where did Steve go?

2. Why did he go there?

3. Did Steve defeat the Wither?

PARTS OF A STORY

> The *setting* is where the story happens. The *plot* is what happens in the story.

*Read the story. Draw a picture that shows the **setting** and **plot** of the story.*

CREEPER TROUBLE

The creeper waits behind a tree in the Forest Biome. There is a ledge nearby. The creeper wants to destroy anything that comes near.

A player comes around the corner. The creeper jumps out. "Ssssay there," the creeper says. "Ssssorry you have to go sssso sssssoon." It explodes and knocks the player off the ledge! Goodbye, player!

INTO THE SWAMP

Read the story. Then draw a picture to show what happened.

ONE HOT DAY AT THE SWAMP

The swamp is a flooded, marsh-like biome in Minecraft. Slimes are hostile mobs that live in the swamp. They like to hop. They attack extremely fast.

One hot day, three frogs hopped into the swamp to cool down. Soon two iron golems felt hot. They wandered into the swamp to cool down. Suddenly, a large slime hopped up out of the swamp! The three frogs and two iron golems moved quickly out of the swamp. They didn't feel hot anymore.

MINING IN MINECRAFT

Read about how to mine in Minecraft. Draw a picture of yourself mining. Make sure to show that you know the tricks of mining.

HOW TO MINE IN MINECRAFT

In order to do well in the Minecraft world, you must learn to mine. Mining is done underground. Make sure to bring food and water with you into the mine. It also helps to have torches and weapons. Mining can be tricky, so it's helpful to know these tricks.

To begin mining, find a cave. There is a lot of coal, iron, and gold in caves. Caves are dark, so you will need some torches. Watch out for hostile mobs! They are hiding everywhere. You will need your weapons to protect you. Also watch for lava. If you fall in lava, you will die.

HOW TO BUILD A SNOW GOLEM

Read how to build a snow golem. Write how building a snow golem and building a snowman are alike and different.

HOW TO BUILD A SNOW GOLEM

To build a snow golem you need a shovel, some snow, a crafting table, and a pumpkin head. With the shovel, punch the snow. Punch the snow until you have eight snowballs. Use a crafting table to make the snowballs into two snow blocks. Put the pumpkin head on top of the two snow blocks. Now you have a snow golem.

How to Build a Snowman

How to Build a Snow Golem

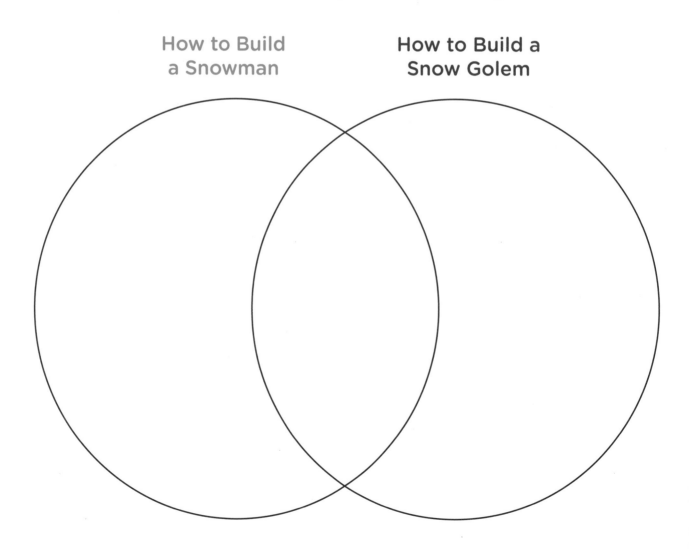

HOW TO TAME A CREEPER

Read about how to tame a creeper. Draw a picture to show how you would tame a creeper.

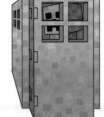

HOW TO TAME A CREEPER

Taming a creeper can be tricky. A creeper does not like to be tamed, but in Minecraft a tamed creeper can be helpful. Follow these steps to tame a creeper.

First, get the creeper into the creeper trap. Next, put one red flower in the corner of the trap. Then, put a yellow flower in the opposite corner of the trap. When you open the trap, your creeper will be tamed.

IN THE DESERT: READ

Read about the Minecraft Desert Biome. Answer the questions on the next page.

ALL ABOUT THE DESERT BIOME

The Desert Biome is made up of sandstone. It is hot in the desert. Some rabbits live in the desert. They hop quickly on the hot sand. Cacti grow in the desert. They are the only green plants in the desert.

In the Minecraft desert you might find a temple. Sometimes you have to dig to find the temple. Temples might be buried under the sand. Inside the temple you might find a chest. It is filled with valuable loot. Be careful. The loot is protected by a TNT trap.

At night the husks spawn in the desert. Husks are like zombies, but husks do not burn in the sun. When a husk dies, it drops rotten flesh.

IN THE DESERT: ANSWER

Answer the questions.

1. What is the Desert Biome made up of?

_____

2. What is the temperature like in the desert?

_____

3. What might you find buried in the sand in the desert?

_____

4. What might you find in a desert temple?

_____

5. What is inside a chest?

_____

6. What does the word **valuable** mean?

_____

7. What mob spawns in the desert?

_____

8. What does a husk drop when it dies?

_____

PLANTS

There are many different types of plants. Find the names of these plants and plant-related words in the word find below.

tree	flower	vegetable	fruit	weed
wheat	cactus	bush	vine	grass

t r i w g r a s s f

r t r e e w n u v l

f e g e t h a b i o

l h s d s e r e n w

v e g e t a b l e e

b u s h o t r n w r

o f r u i t e a t e

w e a t c a c t u s

PARTS OF A PLANT

Label the parts of a plant.

stem	leaf	petal	roots

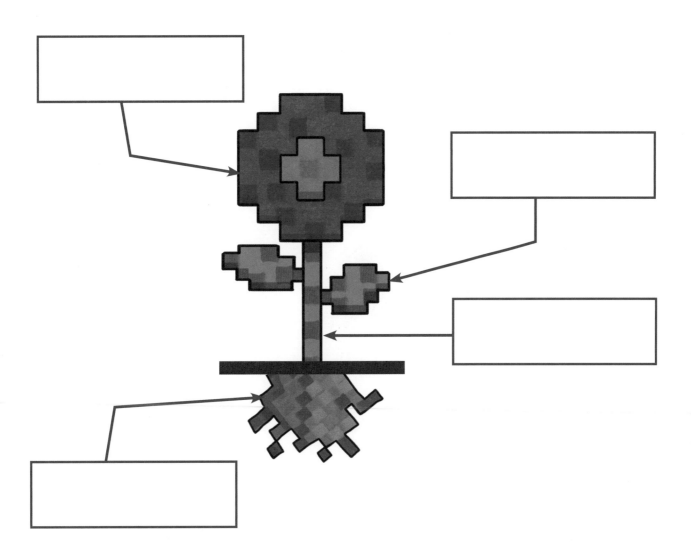

WHAT DO PLANTS NEED TO GROW?

Circle the three things plants need to grow.

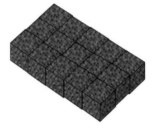

HOW PLANTS GROW

Number the pictures 1 – 6 in the order a plant grows.

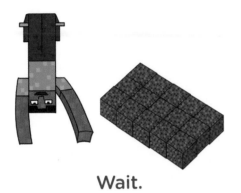

Wait.

Drop a seed in the hole.

Cover the seed with dirt.

Make a hole in the dirt.

Soon you will have a plant.

Water the ground.

WHAT LIVING THINGS NEED

Look at the pictures to see what living things need to survive. Complete the sentences using one of the words provided.

food   water   shelter   sunlight   air

1. Living things need to eat _____ .

2. _____ shines down and helps plants grow.

3. Humans and animals breathe _____ to live.

4. Homes, nests, and caves are different types of _____ .

5. Living things need to drink _____ .

WEATHER FORECAST

Study the forecast. Then answer the questions.

1. Skeletons and zombies burn up in the sunlight. Which three days are most dangerous for them? _____

_____

_____

2. Blazes who make it to the Overworld are damaged by rain. On which days will blazes take damage?_____

_____

3. What is your favorite kind of weather? _____

_____

4. What do you think the weather will be like on Monday? Draw a picture of your prediction in the forecast box.

MY PLATE

When your hunger bar is low, you need to choose healthy foods that give you energy. Look at the foods below. Color the circles next to the fruits red, vegetables green, grains brown, proteins purple, and dairy blue.

Hey, little villager! You need to eat right to grow big like me.

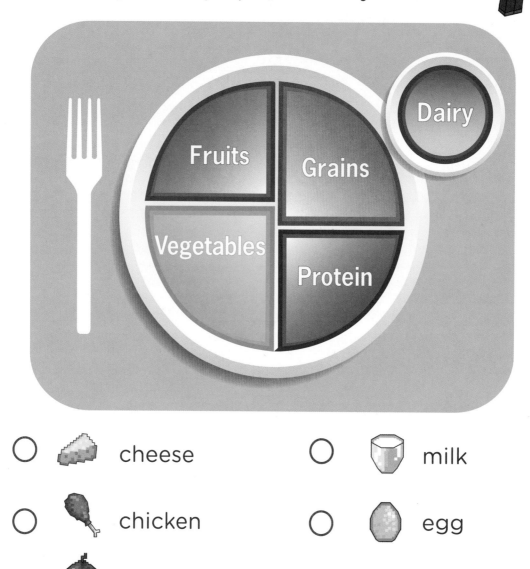

○ cheese ○ milk

○ chicken ○ egg

○ apple ○ potato

○ carrot ○ beef

○ bread ○ melon

HEALTHY FOODS

Complete the crossword.

Nutritious foods give us energy!

| apple | banana | egg | grains |
| milk | meat | nuts | protein |

ACROSS

1 a yellow fruit that needs to be peeled

4 a protein that's hatched

7 meats, eggs, and nuts are part of this food group

8 protein from animals

DOWN

2 a red fruit that's great in pie

3 these are small and tough to crack

5 bread and rice are part of this food group

6 a white dairy drink

GERMS

Read about germs. Then draw a picture showing how you will keep germs from spreading.

Although not poisonous like me, germs can harm you.

Germs are little creatures. They are so small you can't see them. They are on things you touch, like doorknobs and computer keyboards. They are in the air. To keep germs from spreading, you can:

- wash your hands after you play
- cover your mouth when you sneeze or cough
- use a tissue to blow your nose

HOW I KEEP GERMS FROM SPREADING

STAY HEALTHY

Do you know how to stay healthy? Here are six healthy habits. Use the words in the word box to complete the sentences.

I stay healthy by fighting off hostile mobs!

bath	mouth	teeth	hands	sleep	food

1. Wash your ....

2. Cover your .... when you sneeze.

3. Brush your ....

4. Take a ....

5. Eat nutritious ....

6. Get plenty of ....

OUR FIVE SENSES

Write the sense that matches each body part.

> This cake **looks** good and **smells** good. Now, I'll have to see if it tastes good.

| hear   see   touch   taste   smell |

1. I .... with my eyes.

2. I .... with my nose.

3. I .... with my mouth.

4. I .... with my ears.

5. I .... with my fingers.

WRITING FOR MINECRAFTERS

SIMPLE SENTENCES

Read each sentence.
Then answer the questions.

A **sentence** has a subject and a predicate.

A **subject** is the person or thing doing the action.

A **predicate** tells what the person or thing is or does.

Evoker casts spells.

1. *Who casts spells?* _____ (subject)

2. *What does evoker do?* _____ (predicate)

Creeper exploded.

3. *Who exploded?* _____ (subject)

4. *What did creeper do?* _____ (predicate)

Iron golem gave the villager a flower.

5. *Who gave the villager a flower?* _____ (subject)

6. *What did iron golem do?* _____ (predicate)

Blaze is a hostile mob.

7. *Who is a hostile mob?* _____ (subject)

8. *What is blaze?* _____ (predicate)

YOUR OWN SENTENCES

Remember to start the sentences with a capital letter and end with a period.

Choose a subject and a predicate to write a sentence on each line.

SUBJECTS	PREDICATES
ghast	works in the village
the villager	fell off a cliff
ocelot	spawned a kitten
snow golem	shoots fireballs

1. _____

_____

2. _____

_____

3. _____

_____

4. _____

_____

FIX THE SENTENCE

Sentences start with a capital letter and end with a period or question mark.

Copy the sentence. Fix the errors.

1. the snow golem is a mob

_____

2. it has two snow blocks and a pumpkin head

_____

3. it throws snowballs

_____

4. does it melt when it gets hot

_____

5. does it melt in the rain

_____

END PUNCTUATION

Most sentences end with . Exciting sentences end with ! Questions end with ?

Place the correct punctuation at the end of each sentence.

 1. The creeper is about to explode

2. Steve made a new sword

 3. Where is the snow golem

4. What time is it

5. The villagers have many jobs

6. The map shows the way home

 7. The witch is about to throw her potion

8. Steve can run fast

WRITING SENTENCES

Sentences start with a capital letter and end with a period or question mark.

Rearrange the words to write a sentence. Don't forget to start with a capital letter and end with a period.

1.    the   cuts   Steve   cake

_____

2.    dragon   through   flies   blocks

_____

3. 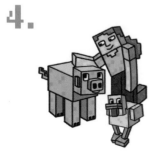   Overworld   in   grow   trees   the

_____

4. 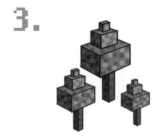   pigs   Alex   and   cares   chickens   for

_____

WRITING SENTENCES

Write sentences about the picture. Use words from the word box.

playground	swing	rings	chalk
play	boy	girl	basketball

1. _____

2. _____

3. _____

4. _____

CAPITALIZATION

Rewrite each sentence using correct capitalization.

Hints: Capitalize the first letter of:
- a sentence
- names
- days and months
- important words in a title

1. alex is a player in the minecraft world.

_____

2. steve wrote a book called <u>mindcraft mining</u>.

_____

3. in april, animals spawn lots of baby animals.

_____

4. on monday, creeper exploded.

_____

5. ender dragon flies around the end.

_____

IN THE DESERT

Read about the Minecraft Desert Biome. Cross out any lowercase letter that should be capitalized. Write the capital letter above. The first one is done for you.

T
~~t~~he Desert Biome is made up of sandstone. it is very dry and hot. very few plants and animals live in the desert. golden rabbits can live there. cacti can live there, too. in some deserts, there may be a desert temple. it is usually buried in the ground. desert temples are dark. in the center of the temple, there is a desert chest. it is filled with valuable loot. at night, husks will spawn in the desert. many players avoid the desert, but not steve. he likes to visit the desert in june when it is really hot. sometimes alex will go with him. they have fun. Sometimes they look for the desert chest.

MIX IT UP

Put the words in these mixed-up sentences in the correct order. Add a capital letter at the beginning of the sentence and a punctuation mark at the end.

1. float sky the in clouds

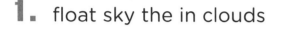

_____

2. hat creeper cowboy a wears the

_____

3. the wins the Enderman race

_____

4. the eats horse carrot a

_____

5. lava watch for the out

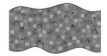

_____

6. fish puffer poisonous are

_____

7. the grow in mushrooms Nether

_____

8. do have not teeth creepers

_____

9. sheep pink dyed this is

_____

10. skeletons mobs hostile are

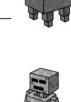

_____

DESCRIBING IN DETAIL

Use the word box on the opposite page to help you write 5 sentences about the picture below. Remember to use capital letters at the beginning of each sentence and a period at the end.

snow   clouds   biome   cold   wildlife

icy   lake   trees   igloo

1. _____

_____

2. _____

_____

3. _____

_____

4. _____

_____

5. _____

_____

DESCRIBING IN DETAIL

Some gamer friends are at the park. Use the word box to help you write 4 sentences about the picture below. Describe the details. Remember to use capital letters at the beginning of each sentence and a period at the end.

basketball	rainbow	slide	swing	trees
climb	sunny	clouds	pavement	chalk

1. _____

_____

_____

2. _____

_____

_____

3. _____

_____

_____

4. _____

_____

_____

SPOT THE VERB

Circle the verb in each sentence.
A verb is the action word in the sentence.

1. Squid shoots ink.

2. Spider crawls up the wall.

3. Steve crafts a sword.

4. Zombie falls into the lava.

SUBJECTS AND VERBS

Write the correct verb.

> When a subject is only one person or thing, add an **s** to the verb.
> *Creeper hides.*
>
> When a subject is more than one, the verb doesn't have an **s**.
> *Creepers hide.*

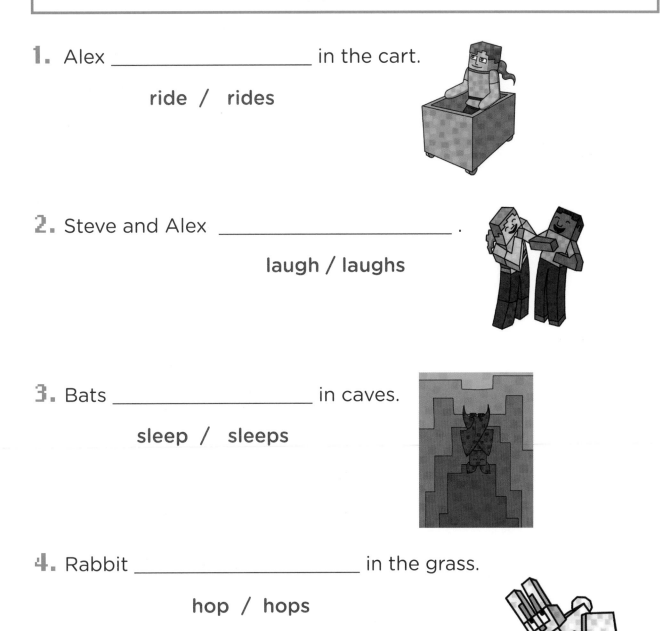

1. Alex _____ in the cart.

ride / rides

2. Steve and Alex _____ .

laugh / laughs

3. Bats _____ in caves.

sleep / sleeps

4. Rabbit _____ in the grass.

hop / hops

CHOOSE THE VERB

Circle the correct verb.

1. Alex **run runs** fast.

2. Cow and the chicken **play plays** with Alex.

3. Alex **fight fights** the dragon.

4. Baby zombie **ride rides** a wolf.

FIX THE SENTENCE

Write the sentence so that the subject and verb go together.

1. The skeletons marches in groups of four.

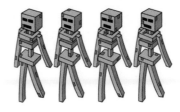

_____

2. The shulker hide in its shell.

_____

3. Nitwit read a map.

_____

4. Alex fight the ghast.

_____

FIND LINKING VERBS

Circle the linking verb in each sentence.

Some verbs don't show action. Verbs that don't show action are linking verbs.

LINKING VERBS					
is	am	are	were	have	has

1. Cow is a passive mob.

2. Baby cows are calves.

3. A mooshroom has mushrooms.

4. Mooblooms have buttercups instead of mushrooms.

WRITE LINKING VERBS

Write the correct linking verb in each sentence.
Use the linking verbs from the box on page 242.

1. Steve _____ upside down.

2. Zombie piglins _____ pink.

3. Skeleton _____ a bow.

4. Ocelots _____ green eyes.

5. "I _____ strong," said Steve.

LINKING VERB TENSES

Write the correct tense of the linking verb in each sentence.
Use the time clues to help.

PRESENT LINKING VERBS	PAST LINKING VERBS
am are is have has	was were had

1. Yesterday Steve _____ fishing.

2. Today Steve _____ exploring.

3. "I _____ going to go mining tomorrow," said Steve.

4. Steve _____ happy when he rode in the cart.

5. The zombies _____ chasing Steve.

LINKING VERBS IN SENTENCES

Write sentences, using a linking verb from the boxes on page 244 to describe each picture.

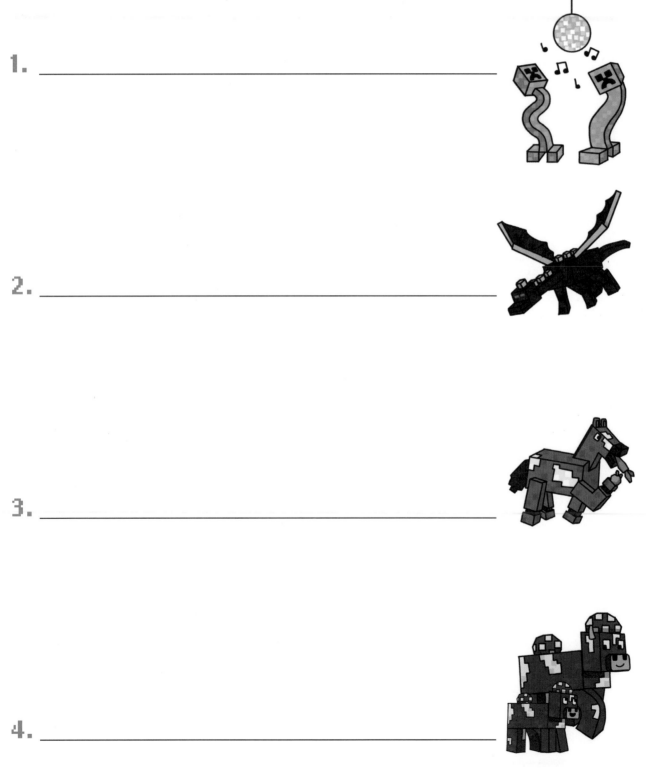

1. _____

2. _____

3. _____

4. _____

TWO FACTS AND AN OPINION

Facts are information that can be proven true.

Read the sentences. Cross out the opinion.

1. Ghast is a white, floating mob.

   Ghast is the meanest mob.

   Ghast is like a jellyfish.

2. Shulkers are box-shaped mobs.

   Shulkers are hostile mobs.

   Shulkers are silly mobs.

3. Zombie piglins are the most dangerous mobs.

   Zombie piglins live mostly in the Nether.

   Zombie piglins spawn with a golden sword.

4. The evoker is very sneaky.

   The evoker casts spells.

   The evoker is an illager.

JUST THE FACTS

Write three facts about each mob. Write the facts in complete sentences.

1. _____

   _____

   _____

2. _____

   _____

   _____

3. _____

   _____

   _____

FACT OR OPINION

Write a fact about each mob.

A fact is something that can be proven to be true.

1. 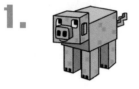 **Example:**

The pig is pink.

....

2.  Steve is

....

3.  The potion is

....

4.  The spider is

....

IN MY OPINION

Which mob is the best one, in your opinion? Write your opinion below and then draw a picture of the mob.

I am the best-looking mob.

That's your opinion.

In my opinion, _____ is the best

mob because _____ .

THE BEST MOB

WRITING SENTENCES

Write a detailed sentence to tell about each picture. Use the words in the boxes to help you.

Nouns		Verbs	
Steve	wolf	exploded	tamed
creeper	Alex	crafted	held
pig	sword	spit	fight
llama	carrot	attacked	defended

 1. _____

_____

 2. _____

_____

 3. _____

_____

 4. _____

_____

WRITING AN OPINION

Who's the best villager—farmer, cleric, librarian, blacksmith, butcher, or nitwit? Fill in the blanks to write your opinion. Give three reasons for your opinion.

In my opinion, _____ is the best villager.

write the name of the villager

One reason is _____ .

write a reason

Another reason is _____ .

write another reason

The last reason is _____ .

write another reason

That is why _____ is the best villager.

write the name of the villager

ADDING DETAILS

Rewrite the sentence, adding adjectives and adverbs to make the sentence more interesting.

Adjectives (describe people and things)			Adverbs (describe actions)		
creepy	huge		slowly	creepily	
dangerous	grumpy	green	quietly	quickly	sneakily

1. The _____ squid swam _____.

....

....

2. The _____ witch _____ made a potion.

....

....

3. The _____ spider crawled _____.

....

....

4. The _____ dragon flew _____.

....

....

ADDING DETAILS

Sentences are made of nouns, verbs, and prepositional phrases. Use the words from each row of the word box to answer the questions. Then, write a complete sentence.

Nouns	Verbs	Prepositional Phrases
1. creeper	exploded	in the village
2. zombie	attacked	in a cave
3. skeleton	spawned	in a pit

1. What? ....

   Did what? ....

   Where? ....

   ....

   ....

2. What? ....

   Did what? ....

   Where? ....

   ....

   ....

3. What? ....

   Did what? ....

   Where? ....

   ....

   ....

CONTRACTIONS

*A **contraction** is two words made shorter by placing an apostrophe where letters have been omitted.*

Example: you are = you're

Write the correct contraction on the space provided. Don't forget the apostrophe!

1. Alex _____ (did not) know what to

do with the diamond.

2. Alex _____ (could not) fit her armor

in the chest.

3. The butcher _____ (was not) able to

sell cooked beef.

4. The spider _____ (can not) attack you

unless you attack it first.

5. _____ (Do not) get too close to a

creeper or it will explode.

MORE CONTRACTIONS

Draw a line connecting each pair of words with its contraction.

1. I am

2. will not

3. could not

4. you are

5. do not

6. we are

7. I would

8. he is

A. we're

B. he's

C. don't

D. won't

E. couldn't

F. I'd

G. you're

H. I'm

SORT THE WORDS

*Sort the words in the box into the columns for nouns, verbs, and adjectives. Remember, a **noun** is a person, place, or thing (like igloo). A **verb** is an action word (like run). An **adjective** is a describing word (like ugly).*

scary	pumpkin	golden	hide	mob
hostile	attack	funny	biome	villager
dig	bird	green	laugh	climb

NOUN	VERB	ADJECTIVE
_____	_____	_____
_____	_____	_____
_____	_____	_____
_____	_____	_____
_____	_____	_____
_____	_____	_____

ADDING DETAILS

*Writing is more interesting when it includes **details**. Change the sentences below. Add details to draw the reader's attention and make the writing more exciting.*

1. The mushroom is red.

_____

_____

2. The snake is scary.

_____

_____

3. Steve is sleeping.

_____

_____

4. The zombie is running away.

_____

_____

WRITING A STORY

Use the characters and setting pictured to write a story.

Characters

Setting

_____

_____

_____

_____

_____

_____

_____

_____

WRITING A STORY

Use the characters, items, and setting pictured to write a story.

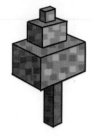

Characters and Items

Setting

_____

_____

_____

_____

_____

_____

_____

WRITE A STORY

Use the characters and setting pictured to write a story.

CHARACTERS

creeper

zombie

Alex

SETTING

Jungle Biome

_____

_____

_____

_____

_____

WRITE A STORY

Use the characters and setting pictured to write a story.

CHARACTERS

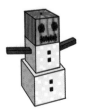

snow golem   bunny

Steve

SETTING

Arctic Biome

_____

_____

_____

_____

_____

WRITING A NARRATIVE

Someone hid a very valuable object in this desert temple. Write a story where you explore this mysterious temple. Describe what you find and what happens next.

Use the sentence starters below for help:

When I walked through the door of the temple, I saw . . .

Next, I . . .

Suddenly, I . . .

Then I . . .

I was shocked that . . .

Finally, I . . .

_____

_____

_____

_____

_____

_____

REVISING MY STORY

All good writers revise their writing. When you revise, you read your writing again to make it better. Use this checklist to revise one of the stories you wrote on pages 258–265.

Answer the questions. If you can't answer yes, revise your writing until you can.

1. Does your story have a beginning that makes

    the reader want to read? _____

2. Does your story have interesting characters? _____

3. Does your story have a clear setting? _____

4. Does your story have a problem that needs to be solved?

    _____

5. Does your story have an ending that solves the problem?

    _____

6. Does your story include interesting details? _____

Rewrite your story on the computer or on another sheet of paper.

EDITING MY STORY

After you have revised your story, it's time to edit. When you edit, you make sure that your story is easy to read. Use this checklist to edit your story from page 266.

☐ I have reread my story, and it makes sense.

☐ Every sentence has a capital letter.

☐ All proper nouns begin with a capital letter.

☐ The title of my story has capital letters.

☐ Every sentence ends with the correct punctuation.

☐ All of the words are spelled correctly.

☐ My subjects and verbs go together.

Read your story to a friend or family member.

INFORMATIONAL WRITING

Writing is a great way to share what you know about a topic. Informational writing can include facts, definitions, and details. It can also have a conclusion. Look at the picture below of the Forest Biome. Pretend you are explaining what the Forest Biome is to someone who has never played Minecraft. Use the sentence starters to help you organize your thoughts.

The Forest Biome is _____

_____

_____ .

The definition of a biome is _____

_____

_____ .

Another interesting fact is _____

_____

_____ .

In conclusion, _____

_____

_____ .

WRITING TO INFORM

Think about a topic you know about or would like to learn about. Write to tell others about the topic. Use the outline to plan your writing.

Topic: _____

Introductory Sentence: _____

_____

_____

Fact 1: _____

Detail: _____

Fact 2: _____

Detail: _____

Fact 3: _____

Detail: _____

Concluding Sentence: _____

_____

_____

WRITING TO INFORM

Use the outline from page 270 to write about the topic.

_____

_____

_____

_____

_____

_____

_____

_____

_____

_____

_____

MINECRAFT RHYMES

Rhymes are short poems. Each line ends in a word that rhymes. Complete each rhyme.

Creeper is a hostile _____

who thinks exploding is its _____ .

To kill a creeper you must _____

where to find an arrow and _____ .

The icky, creepy spider climbed up the dungeon _____ .

Until the clever player made the spider _____ .

The icky, creepy spider was far above Alex's _____ ,

as the player was asleep, comfy in his _____ .

Your turn! Write a rhyme about your favorite Minecraft mob.

_____

_____

MINECRAFT ACROSTICS

An acrostic is a type of poem created by using each letter of a word to describe the word. Read the acrostic about Creeper. Then write your own acrostics.

Use a dictionary to help you find words and look up words you don't know.

COOL
RUTHLESS
EXPLOSIVE
EXCITING
POWERFUL
ENERGETIC
REBELLIOUS

P _____
I _____
G _____

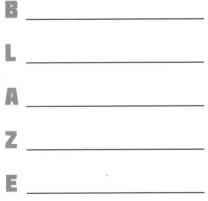

B _____
L _____
A _____
Z _____
E _____

Write Your Own

_____ _____

_____ _____

_____ _____

_____ _____

_____ _____

_____ _____

MINECRAFT HAIKU

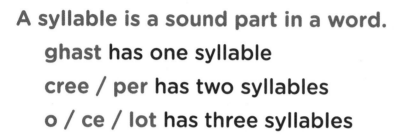

A haiku is a three-line poem that uses syllable patterns. Read the haiku poem. Then write your own about one of your favorite mobs.

A syllable is a sound part in a word.

    ghast has one syllable

    cree / per has two syllables

    o / ce / lot has three syllables

Haiku Syllable Pattern

five syllables	ocelots are cool
seven syllables	found in all kinds of jungles
five syllables	they are super-fast

Write Your Own

_____

_____

_____

DIAMOND POEM

Read the diamond poem. Diamond poems compare two opposites. Write your own diamond poem about a hostile and a passive mob.

Creeper
green, deadly
exploding, killing, screeching
TNT, gunpowder, eggs, chicks
flapping, laying, clucking
white, aimless
Chicken

A hostile mob	_____
Two adjectives describing the hostile mob	_____ , _____
Three "ing" words describing the hostile mob	_____ , _____ , _____
Four nouns: first two relate to the hostile mob and second two relate to a passive mob	_____ , _____ , _____ , _____
Three "ing" words describing the passive mob	_____ , _____ , _____
Two adjectives describing the passive mob	_____ , _____
The passive mob	_____

MINECRAFT COMIC STRIPS

Write what the mobs might be saying to each other. Add talk bubbles. Make it funny. The first one is done for you.

MORE MINECRAFT COMIC STRIPS

Draw your own!

PUZZLES AND GAMES FOR MINECRAFTERS

FIND THE DIFFERENCES

List the differences you see in these pictures.
Find at least 8.

_____

_____

_____

_____

_____

_____

_____

_____

Use the decoder to solve the riddle.

DECODER

A	B	C	D	E	F	G	H	I	J	K	L	M
6	22	12	25	20	8	1	23	14	18	10	2	19

N	O	P	Q	R	S	T	U	V	W	X	Y	Z
26	7	3	24	13	21	16	4	15	9	17	5	11

Why don't witches in the Minecraft world fly on brooms?

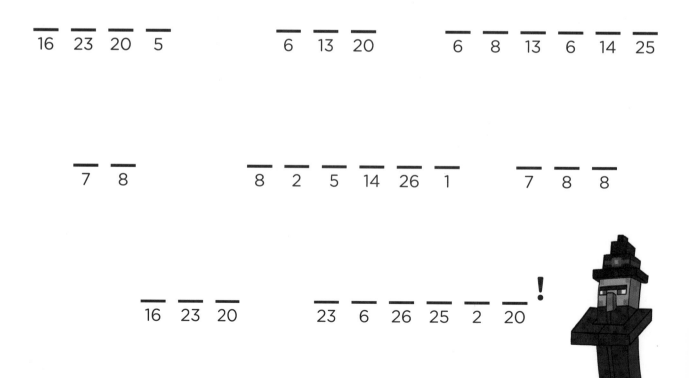

T H E Y   A R E   A F R A I D
16 23 20 5   6 13 20   6 8 13 6 14 25

O F   F L Y I N G   O F F
7 8   8 2 5 14 26 1   7 8 8

T H E   H A N D L E !
16 23 20   23 6 26 25 2 20

WITHER OR WITCH WORDS

Write the words you can spell using the letters in the words **wither** *and* **witch**.

WITHER

WITCH

with

it

CRACK THE CODE 2

Use the decoder to solve the riddle.

DECODER												
A	B	C	D	E	F	G	H	I	J	K	L	M
6	22	12	25	20	8	1	23	14	18	10	2	19
N	O	P	Q	R	S	T	U	V	W	X	Y	Z
26	7	3	24	13	21	16	4	15	9	17	5	11

Why didn't the zombie go to the party?

$\underset{14}{\_\_}\ \underset{16}{\_\_}\qquad \underset{9}{\_\_}\ \underset{6}{\_\_}\ \underset{21}{\_\_}\qquad \underset{8}{\_\_}\ \underset{20}{\_\_}\ \underset{20}{\_\_}\ \underset{2}{\_\_}\ \underset{14}{\_\_}\ \underset{26}{\_\_}\ \underset{1}{\_\_}$

$\underset{13}{\_\_}\ \underset{7}{\_\_}\ \underset{16}{\_\_}\ \underset{16}{\_\_}\ \underset{20}{\_\_}\ \underset{26}{\_\_}.$

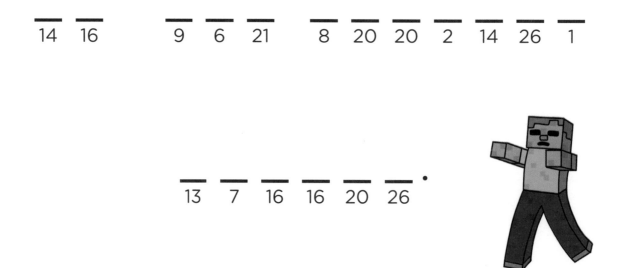

GOLEM VS. GOLEM

Write the words you can spell using the letters in the words **iron golem** *and* **snow golem**.

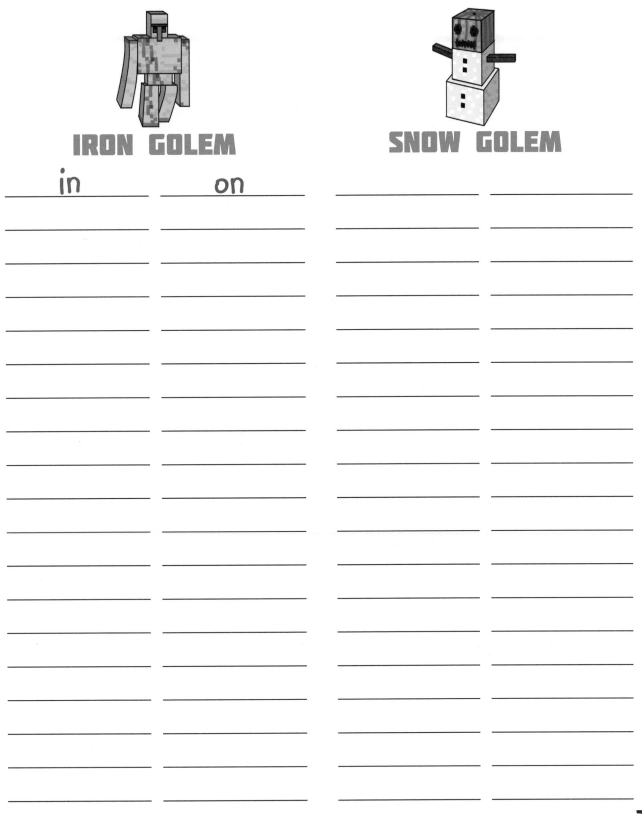

IRON GOLEM   **SNOW GOLEM**

in   on

FROM BOW TO BAT

Read the clues. Change one letter to get from bow to bat.

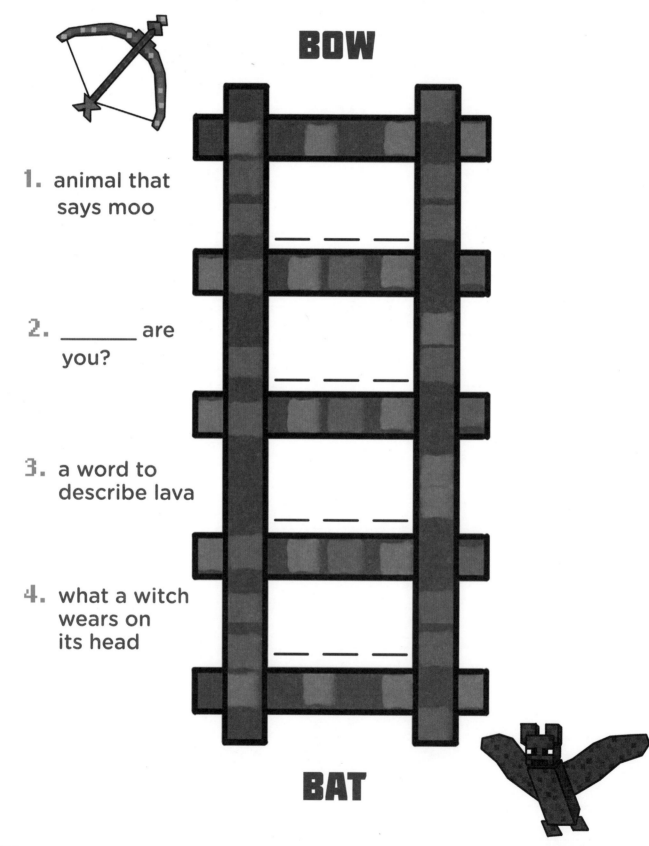

BOW

1. animal that says moo

2. _____ are you?

3. a word to describe lava

4. what a witch wears on its head

BAT

PAIR UP THE MOBS

Circle the two mobs who don't have a match.

FROM GHAST TO CAT

Read the clues. Change one letter to get from ghast to cat.

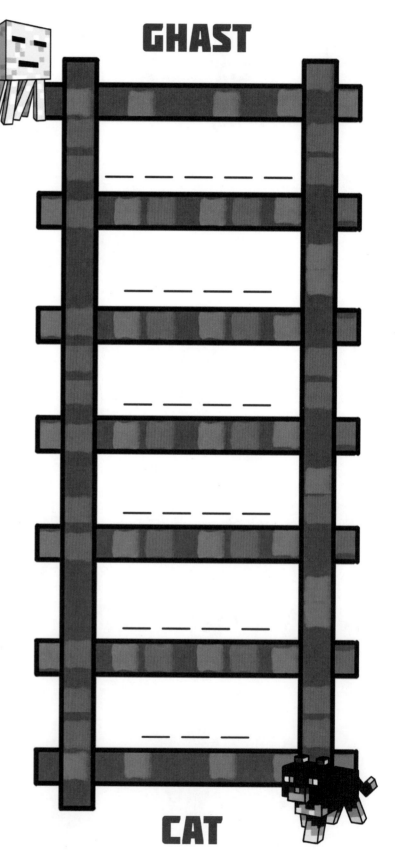

GHAST

1. **add a letter**
   white and spooky
   character

   _ _ _ _ _ _

2. **drop a letter**
   throw a party

   _ _ _ _

3. **change a letter**
   opposite of found

   _ _ _ _

4. **change a letter**
   opposite of first

   _ _ _ _

5. **change a letter**
   opposite of slow

   _ _ _ _

6. **drop a letter**
   opposite of thin

   _ _ _

CAT

PAIR UP THE BLOCKS

Circle the two blocks that don't have a match.

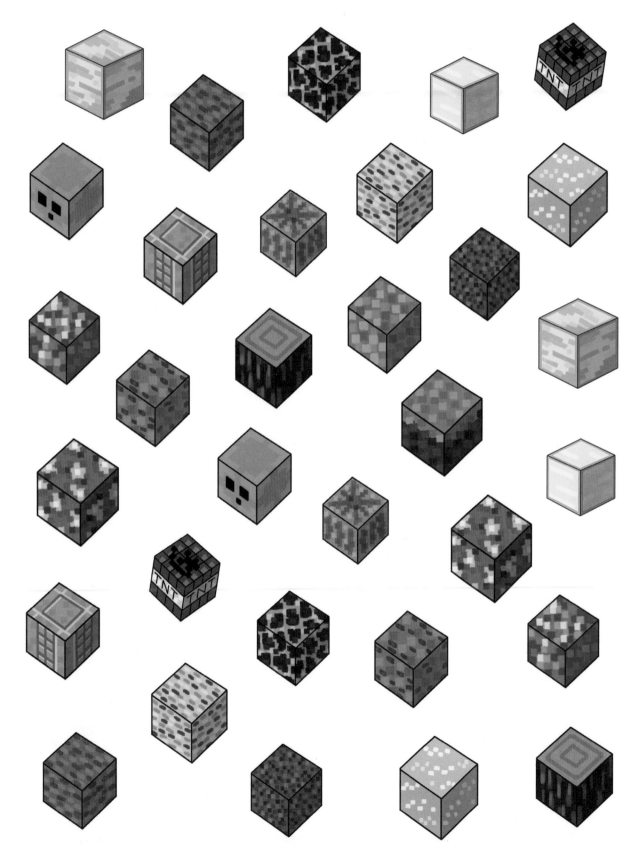

CRACK THE CODE 3

Use the decoder to solve the riddle.

DECODER

A	B	C	D	E	F	G	H	I	J	K	L	M
6	22	12	25	20	8	1	23	14	18	10	2	19

N	O	P	Q	R	S	T	U	V	W	X	Y	Z
26	7	3	24	13	21	16	4	15	9	17	5	11

What did snow golem need when he bumped his head?

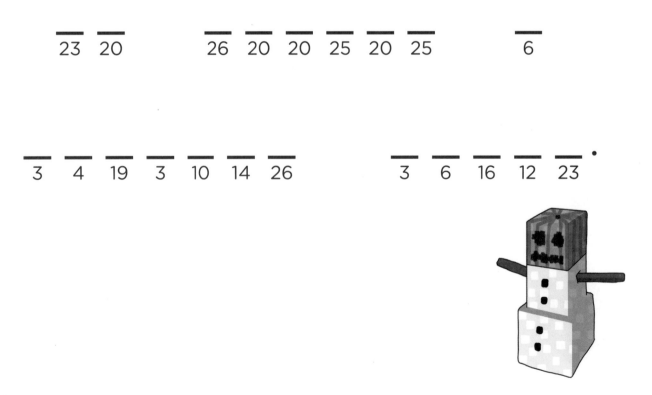

$\overline{}\ \overline{}$
23 20

$\overline{}\ \overline{}\ \overline{}\ \overline{}\ \overline{}\ \overline{}$
26 20 20 25 20 25

$\overline{}$
6

$\overline{}\ \overline{}\ \overline{}\ \overline{}\ \overline{}\ \overline{}\ \overline{}$
3 4 19 3 10 14 26

$\overline{}\ \overline{}\ \overline{}\ \overline{}\ \overline{}$.
3 6 16 12 23

DIAMOND OR EMERALD?

*Write the words you can spell using the letters in the words **diamond** and **emerald**.*

DIAMOND

EMERALD

_____and_____   _____it_____   _____   _____

_____   _____   _____   _____

_____   _____   _____   _____

_____   _____   _____   _____

_____   _____   _____   _____

_____   _____   _____   _____

_____   _____   _____   _____

_____   _____   _____   _____

CRACK THE CODE 4

Use the decoder to solve the riddle.

DECODER

A	B	C	D	E	F	G	H	I	J	K	L	M
6	22	12	25	20	8	1	23	14	18	10	2	19

N	O	P	Q	R	S	T	U	V	W	X	Y	Z
26	7	3	24	13	21	16	4	15	9	17	5	11

Why did Steve mine in the garden for gold?

‾‾ ‾‾   ‾‾ ‾‾ ‾‾ ‾‾ ‾‾ ‾‾   ‾‾ ‾‾   ‾‾ ‾‾ ‾‾ ‾‾
23 20   9 6 26 16 20 25   16 7   8 14 26 25

‾‾ ‾‾   ‾‾ ‾‾ ‾‾ ‾‾ ‾‾ ‾‾ ‾‾   ‾‾ ‾‾ ‾‾ ‾‾ .
G U   12 6 13 13 7 16 21   1 7 2 25

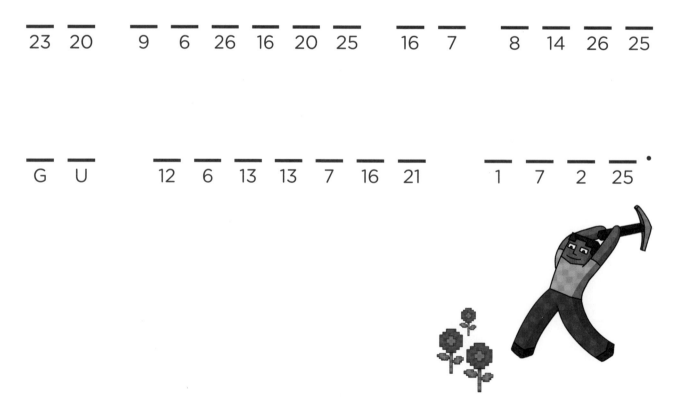

290

LIBRARIAN VS. ENDERMAN

Write the words you can spell using the letters in the words **librarian** *and* **enderman**.

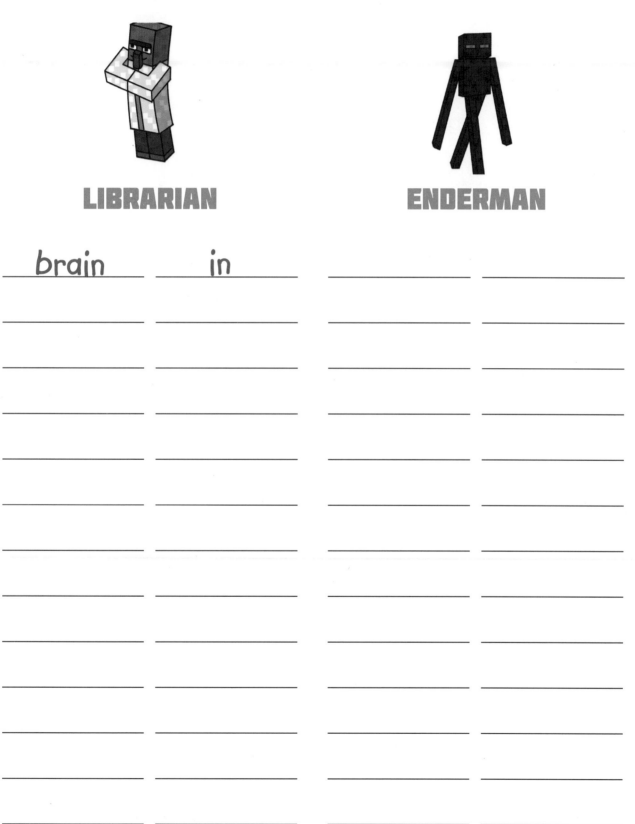

LIBRARIAN   **ENDERMAN**

brain   in

HIDDEN TAPPABLES 1

An icon is tappable if it appears in all four boxes. Only two of the below items appear in every box. Can you find and circle the two tappables before they despawn?

MOB DROPS

Four Minecraft Earth players collected special mob variants today. Follow the paths under and over crossing paths to discover which mob dropped into which player's inventory.

WOOLY COW   CLUCKSHROOM   JUMBO RABBIT   JOLLY LLAMA

TRISHENANIGAN   JANA   CL LOVES

STEFFEEFEE   BANANA   GREEN

FUNNY FOOD

Build a crossword on this buildplate. Use the picture clues to guess the word answers, then figure out where each word logically fits. Transfer the numbered letters to the spaces with the same numbers. If you fill in the puzzle correctly, you'll get funny answers to the questions below.

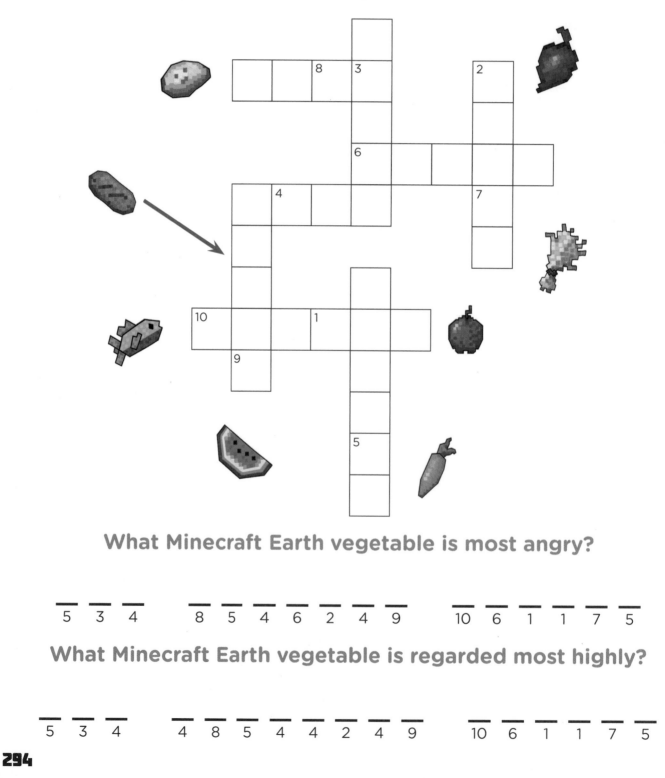

What Minecraft Earth vegetable is most angry?

$\overline{5}$ $\overline{3}$ $\overline{4}$ $\overline{8}$ $\overline{5}$ $\overline{4}$ $\overline{6}$ $\overline{2}$ $\overline{4}$ $\overline{9}$ $\overline{10}$ $\overline{6}$ $\overline{1}$ $\overline{1}$ $\overline{7}$ $\overline{5}$

What Minecraft Earth vegetable is regarded most highly?

$\overline{5}$ $\overline{3}$ $\overline{4}$ $\overline{4}$ $\overline{8}$ $\overline{5}$ $\overline{4}$ $\overline{4}$ $\overline{2}$ $\overline{4}$ $\overline{9}$ $\overline{10}$ $\overline{6}$ $\overline{1}$ $\overline{1}$ $\overline{7}$ $\overline{5}$

FREE FOR THE TAPPING

Read the three clues below to identify which of the nine items is tappable. Circle it and tap away!

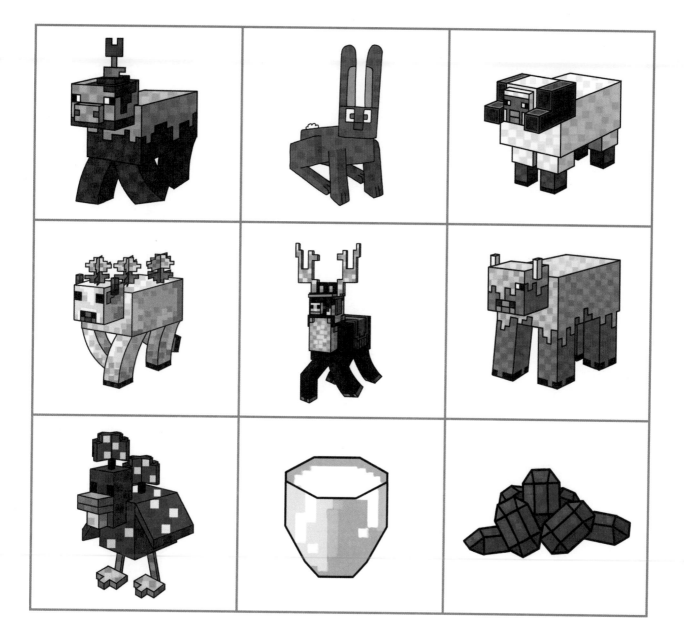

CLUES:

1. The tappable icon is either in the top row, the right column, or the center square.

2. The tappable icon is not in a corner square.

3. The tappable icon is not a woolly cow or a jolly llama.

CAPTURE THE MOOBLOOM

Warning: This maze will have you running around in circles like a Cluckshroom in direct sunlight! If you can avoid the creeper and get to the Moobloom, it's yours!

A JOLLY GOOD FRIEND

Get the hostile skeletons before they get you! Kill the right ones, and you can add a good joke to your inventory.

Here are the rules: Wipe out every skeleton above a llama, directly to the left of a sheep block, or below a chicken. Write letters from the remaining skeletons on the spaces to reveal the answer to the joke.

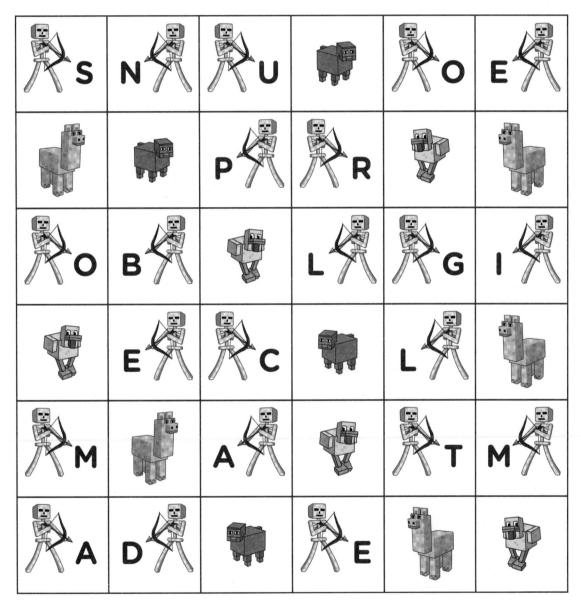

What does a Jolly Llama say when you ask him for a favor?

__ __ __ __ __ __ __ — __ __ __ __ __

HIDDEN TAPPABLES 2

An icon is tappable if it appears in all four boxes. Only two of the below items appear in every box. Can you find and circle the two tappables before they despawn?

GROUP ADVENTURE: FOUR FOR ORE

Four Minecraft Earth players are sharing an adventure in a local park, looking to mine some diamonds. Follow each player's path, under and over crossing paths, to discover who, if anyone, reaches the diamond ore.

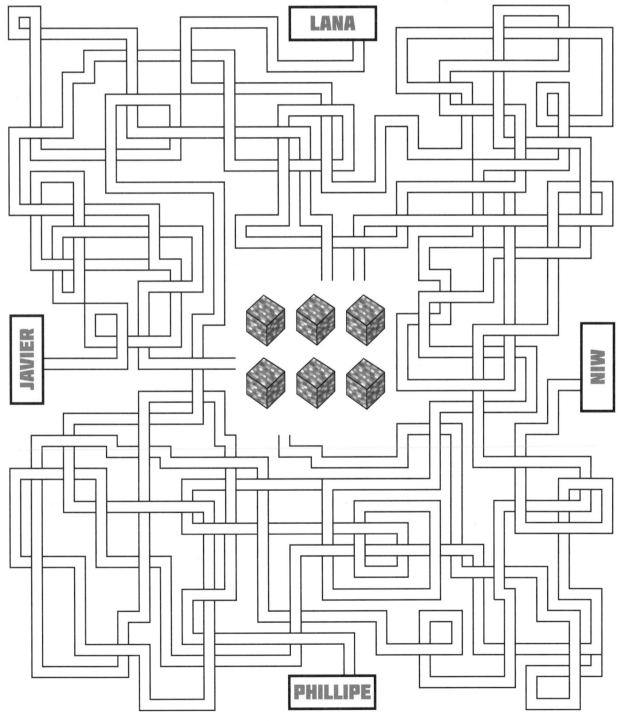

LANA

JAVIER

NIW

PHILLIPE

HUSHED CROWD

Build a crossword on this buildplate. Use the picture clues to guess the word answers, then figure out where each word logically fits. Transfer the numbered letters to the spaces with the same numbers. If you fill in the puzzle correctly, you'll get a funny answer to the question below.

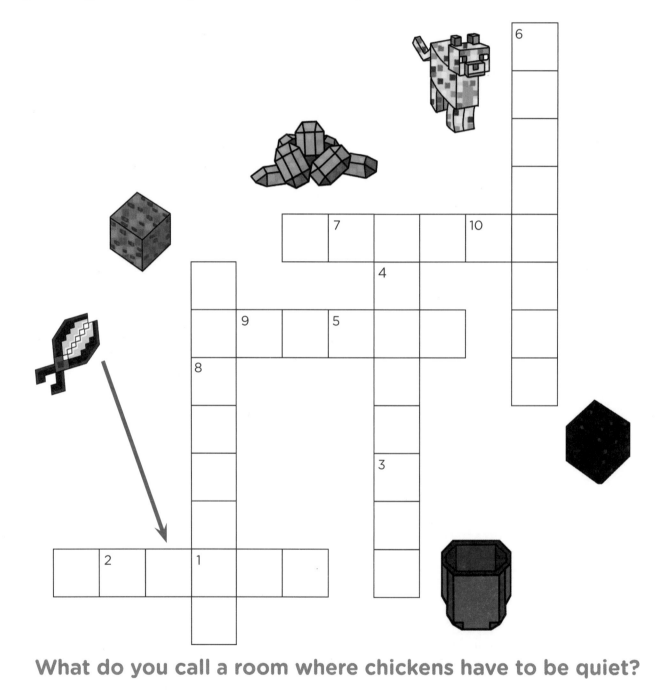

What do you call a room where chickens have to be quiet?

— — — — — — — — — — — —
1   7   3   9   7   5   8   2   6   10   10   4

TRICKY TRICK KEY

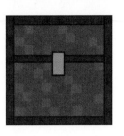

The key to opening this chest is tapping one of the icons below. Follow the three clues below to decide which of the nine icons is tappable. Circle the icon when you figure it out, and tap away!

CLUES:

1. The tappable icon is either in a corner square or the middle row.

2. The tappable icon is not the torch or in line with the torch, vertically or horizontally.

3. The tappable icon is not mined or planted.

BEACON BOUND

There's a Minecraft Earth adventure beacon on your screen. You're armed and ready to battle mobs, mine, and search for treasure. Can you find your way through these crazy city streets to reach the adventure?

START

FINISH

PASSED OVER PASSIVE MOB

Cross off every mob above a block of grass, to the right of a tree, and between two diagonal red mushrooms. Write letters from the remaining mobs on the spaces to answer the riddle.

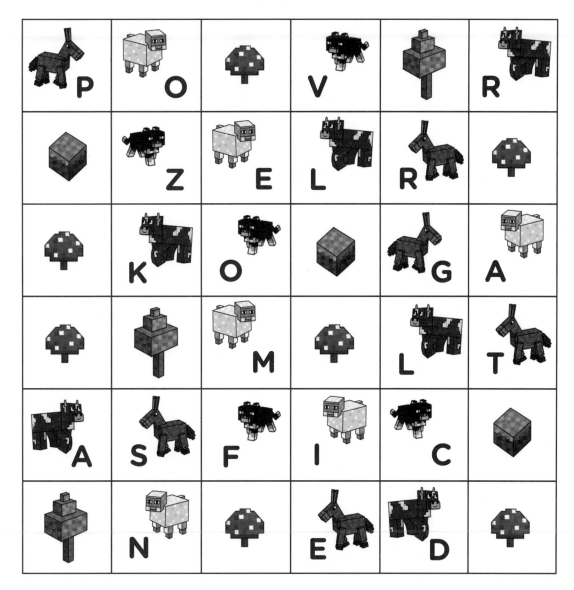

What peaceful animal was passed over as a passive mob for Minecraft Earth?

We can't tell you, but here's a hint:

Game developers thought it was _____ .

__ __ __ __ __ __ – __ __ __ __ __ __ __ __ __ __ – __ __ __ __

HIDDEN TAPPABLES 3

Two of the items in the boxes below are tappables. An icon is tappable if it appears in all four boxes. Can you find and circle the two tappables before they despawn?

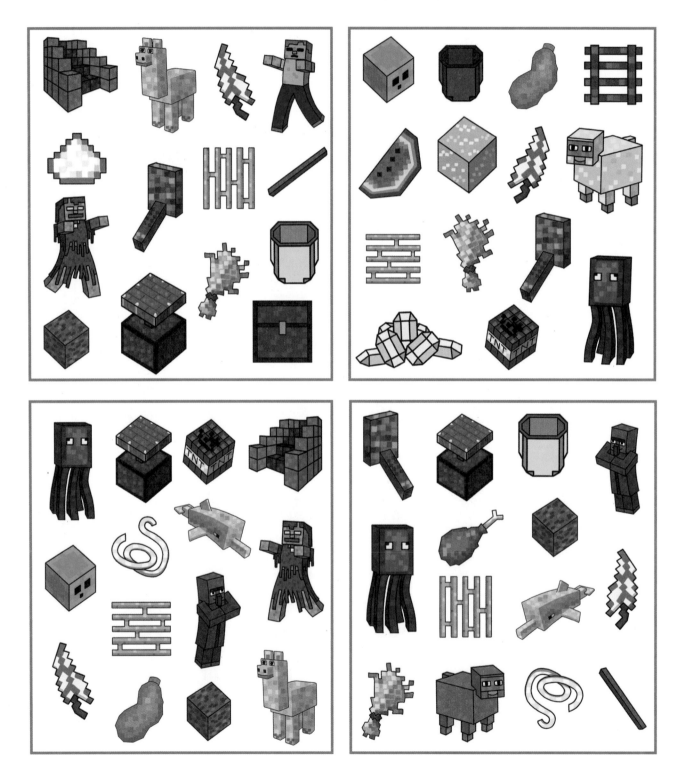

LLAMA DRAMA

Four players are racing to claim the Jolly Llama for their Minecraft Earth inventories. Follow each player's path under and over crossing paths to discover who finds the holiday-themed llama variant.

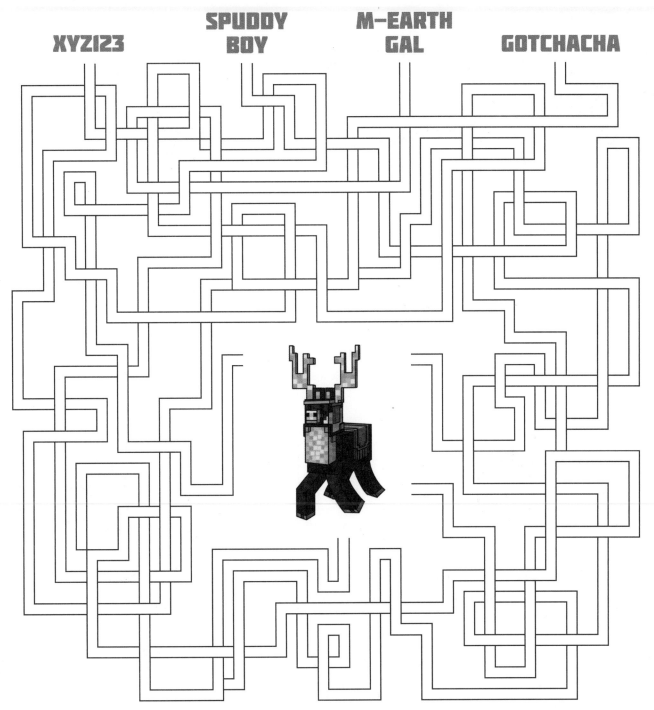

XYZ123   SPUDDY BOY   M-EARTH GAL   GOTCHACHA

BUILT TO LAST

Use the picture clues to guess the word answers, then figure out where each word logically fits. Transfer the numbered letters to the spaces with the same numbers to answer the riddle.

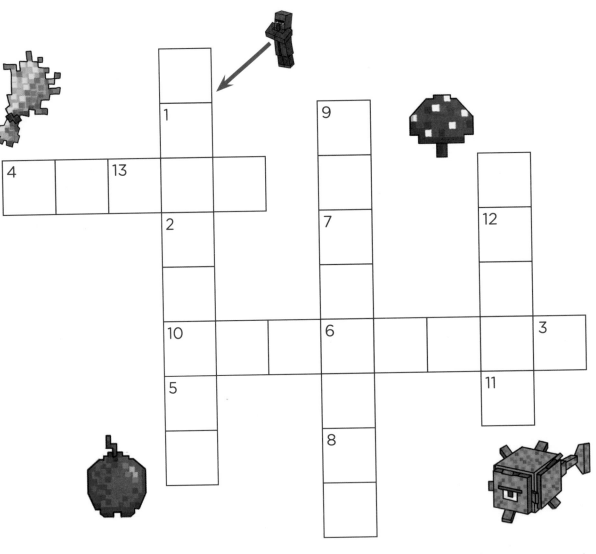

To make something you build last so that others can enjoy it, turn it into this:

$\overline{}_{4}$ $\overline{}_{13}$ $\overline{}_{5}$ $\overline{}_{6}$ $\overline{}_{7}$ $\overline{}_{1}$ $\overline{}_{7}$ $\overline{}_{11}$ $\overline{}_{5}$ $\overline{}_{3}$ $\overline{}_{11}$

$\overline{}_{12}$ $\overline{}_{8}$ $\overline{}_{2}$ $\overline{}_{8}$ $\overline{}_{10}$ $\overline{}_{6}$ $\overline{}_{4}$ $\overline{}_{9}$

SECRET SPELUNKING ENTRANCE

Who's up for some spelunking? To enter the cave and start this Minecraft Earth puzzle adventure, you must tap one of the icons below. Follow the clues and circle the icon that is tappable.

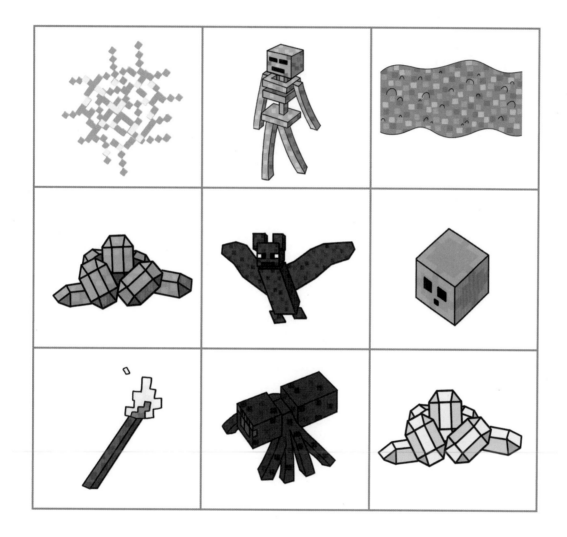

CLUES:

1. The tappable icon is either a gem or a mob.

2. The tappable icon is either in the top row or the center column, but not both.

3. The tappable icon is never hostile.

RUBY QUEST

Find your way through this maze from Start to the Ruby treasure. Cha-ching!

START

MOST SPECIAL MOB

Cross out and destroy every hostile mob to the right of a block. Then cross out mobs between two flowers horizontally or vertically (not diagonally). Write letters from the remaining mobs on the spaces to reveal the answer to this question:

What was the rarest mob to drop from a tappable chest in the early days of Minecraft Earth?

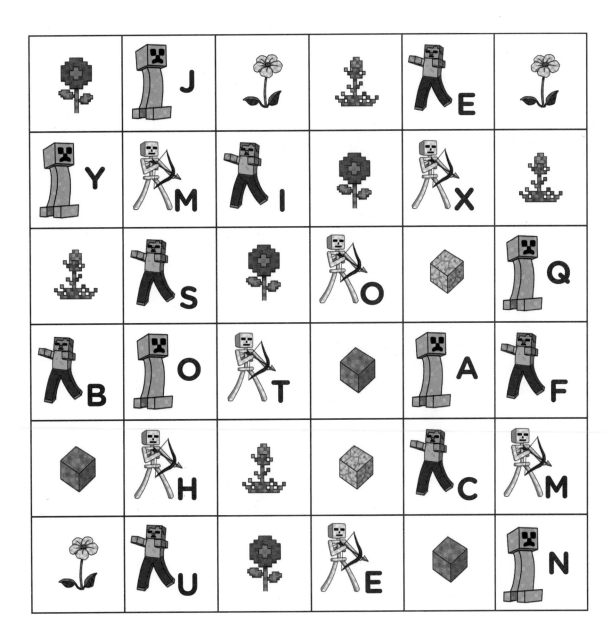

___ ___ ___ ___ ___ ___ ___ ___ ___

HIDDEN TAPPABLES 4

Two of the items in the boxes below are tappables. An icon is tappable if it appears in all four boxes. Can you find and circle the two tappables before they despawn?

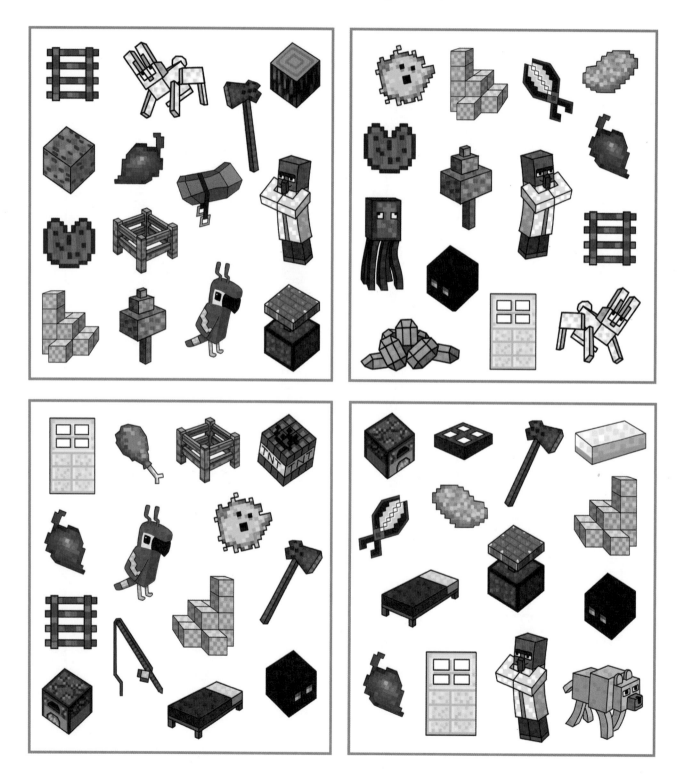

ARCTIC ADVENTURE

You invited four Minecraft Earth friends on an arctic adventure. Follow each friend's path, under and over crossing paths, to discover which friends joined you in the arctic.

MINDY   **MAX**   **MIA**   **MILTON**

OCELOTS RULE

Build a crossword on this buildplate. Use the picture clues to guess the word answers, then figure out where each word logically fits. Transfer the numbered letters to the spaces with the same numbers. If you fill in the puzzle correctly, you'll reveal the answer to the joke.

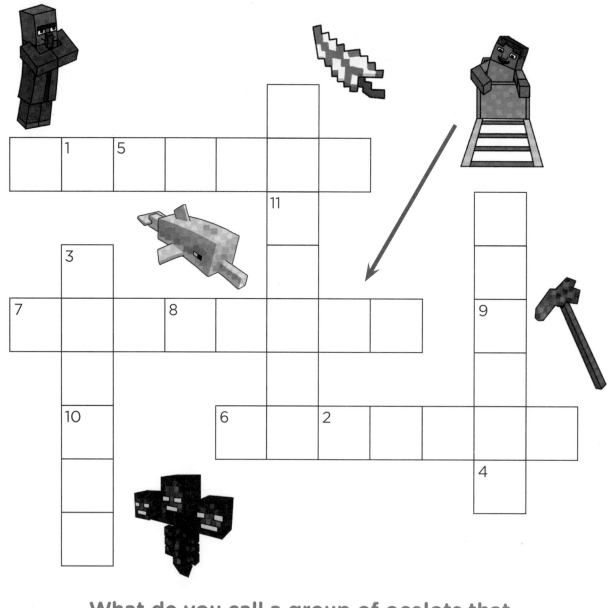

What do you call a group of ocelots that keep the peace in Minecraft Earth?

$\overline{11}\ \overline{5}\ \overline{2}\ \overline{10}\qquad \overline{8}\ \overline{3}\ \overline{6}\ \overline{1}\ \overline{4}\ \overline{11}\ \overline{8}\ \overline{7}\ \overline{8}\ \overline{3}\ \overline{9}$

ON YOUR MARK, GET SET, TAP, GO!

One of your clever Minecraft Earth friends has built a cool redstone chain reaction device. To start it, you have to tap one of the icons in the grid. If you tap the wrong icon, the device locks. Use the clues to figure out which item needs to be tapped, and circle it to start the chain reaction.

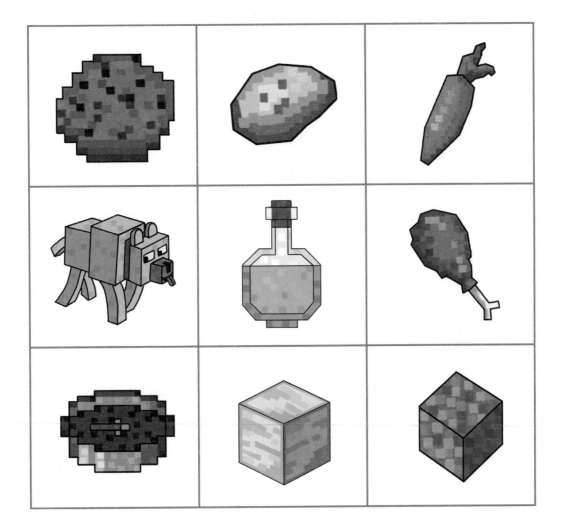

CLUES:

1. The tappable item is either a good building tool or a pet.

2. The tappable icon is directly below something edible.

3. The tappable icon is either in the bottom row or the center column.

ROUND 'EM UP!

Catch these exclusive Minecraft Earth farm mobs as you find your way through this maze from START to FINISH.

START

FINISH

MOUNTAIN MERRIMENT

Cross out every llama to the left of or below a silverfish. Then cross out every llama to the right of or above emeralds. Write letters from the remaining llamas on the spaces to fill in the blanks and answer the joke.

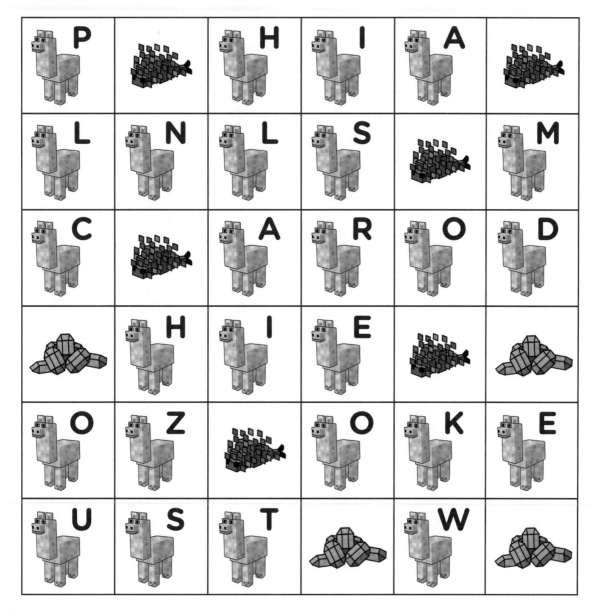

Why can't you wander through mountain biomes without laughing your head off?

Because they're H I L L ___ ___ ___ ___ ___ ___ ___ **.**

—

HILL-ARIOUS

HIDDEN TAPPABLES 5

Two of the items in the boxes below are tappables. An icon is tappable if it appears in all four boxes. Can you find and circle the two tappables before they despawn?

QR QUEST

A life-sized statue of a moobloom was placed in a local park. Six friends hope to reach it, click the QR code, and receive a special, secret drop. Follow each player's path, under and over crossing paths, to discover which players, if any, find the life-sized moobloom.

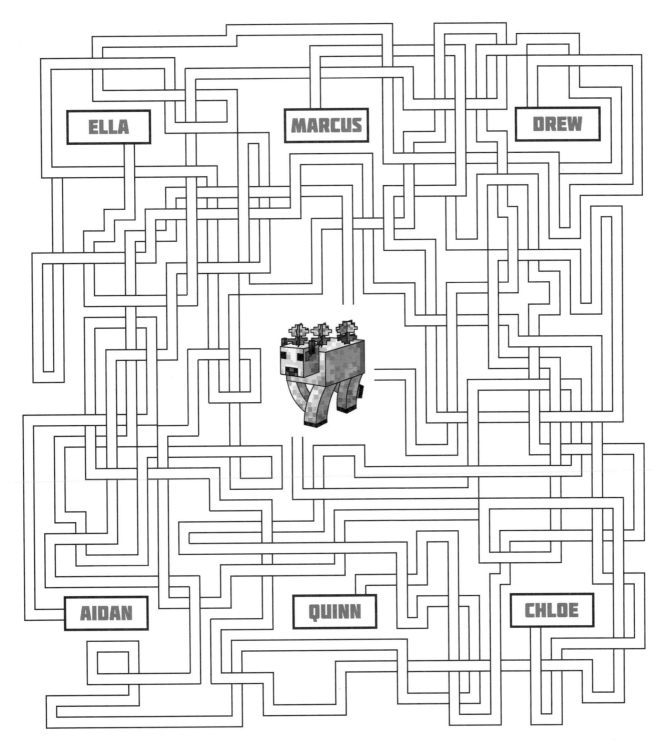

THE NAME OF THE GAME

Build a crossword on this buildplate. Use the picture clues to guess the word answers, then figure out where each word logically fits. Transfer the numbered letters to the spaces with the same numbers to answer the riddle.

What kind of game is Minecraft Earth?

__ __ __ __ __ __ __ __ __   __ __ __ __ __ __ __
12 7 10 3 5 9 6 5 2   11 5 12 4 1 6 8

CEASE FIRE!

Escape hostile mobs by using the clues to discover which one of the icons below is tappable. If you tap the wrong icon, you're on your own with the mobs. If you tap the right icon, they will all despawn. Circle the icon that is tappable.

CLUES:

1. The tappable icon is either in the middle row or a corner square.

2. The tappable icon is a mob.

3. The tappable icon is to the right of a lava river.

HIDDEN TAPPABLES 6

Two of the items in the boxes below are tappables. An icon is tappable if it appears in all four boxes. Can you find and circle the two tappables before they despawn?

FINDERS KEEPERS

Four Minecraft Earth friends are about to be rewarded for adventuring. Follow each player's path, under and over crossing paths, to discover who gets what.

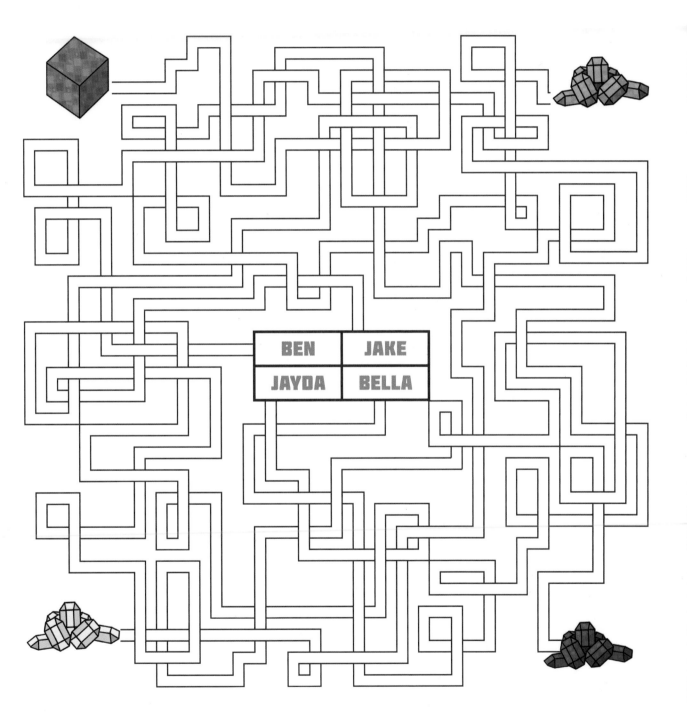

COOKING UP CLUES

Use the picture clues to guess the word answers, then figure out where each word logically fits. Transfer the numbered letters to the spaces with the same numbers. If you fill in the puzzle correctly, you'll discover a fun fact about Adventures.

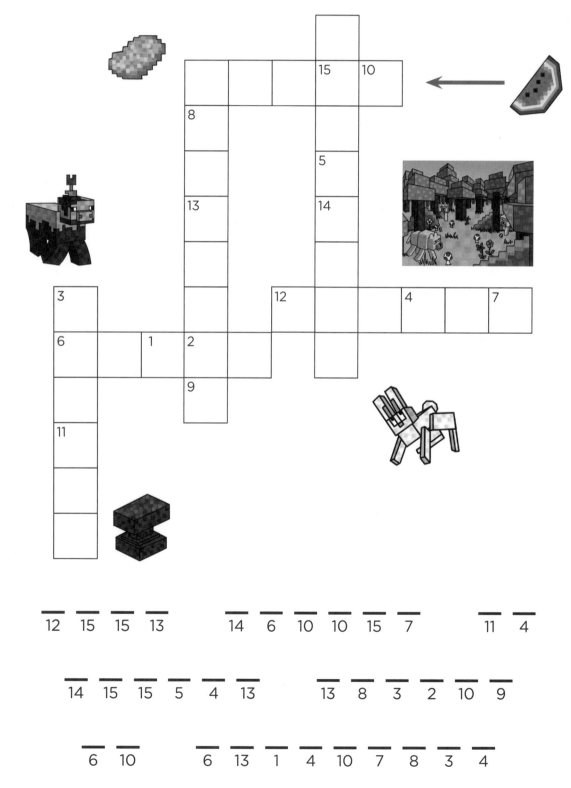

15   10

8

5

13   14

3   12   4   7

6   1   2

9

11

___ ___ ___ ___   ___ ___ ___ ___ ___ ___   ___ ___
12 15 15 13   14   6 10 10 15   7   11   4

___ ___ ___ ___ ___ ___   ___ ___ ___ ___ ___ ___
14 15 15   5   4 13   13   8   3   2 10   9

___ ___   ___ ___ ___ ___ ___ ___ ___ ___ ___
 6 10   6 13   1   4 10   7   8   3   4

TRUE FRIENDS

Your friends are waiting to play Minecraft Earth with you on the other side of this maze.

Can you find your way from START to FINISH? It will be easier if you correctly identify each statement as true or false.

START

False

True

Uninvited players can collect resources from your Minecraft Earth pinned world.

True

Only one player at a time can interact with a Minecraft Earth Adventure buildplate.

False

False

True

Use QR codes to invite friends to play with you locally.

FINISH

ARROW ADVENTURE

To complete this maze adventure, you must follow the arrows. If you can find the path that leads from START to FINISH and avoids the creepers, you can claim ten rubies and lots of experience points! If there are two arrows in a square, you can choose to go either direction.

START   FINISH

MUDDY PIG RUNNING AMOK

Can you catch the muddy pig? The word muddy pig appears only once (forward or backward) in a horizontal, vertical, or diagonal line. If you find it, circle it!

D G I P Y M M U G P

U Y G D D U M M U M

M M I M M D U D M M

M U P M D Y D I U G

Y D Y Y P I G D D I

P P D D N M Y Y D Y

I M D G P P P D Y D

G M U D I I I D G D

M U M G P G G U I U

G U P Y D D U M P M

NAVIGATIONAL HAZARDS

There are mobs to be fought and gems to be mined on the other side of this maze! Follow the arrows to complete the Minecraft Earth adventure. If there are two arrows in a box, you can choose to go either direction. Can you avoid the lava and get out in fighting condition?

START   **FINISH**

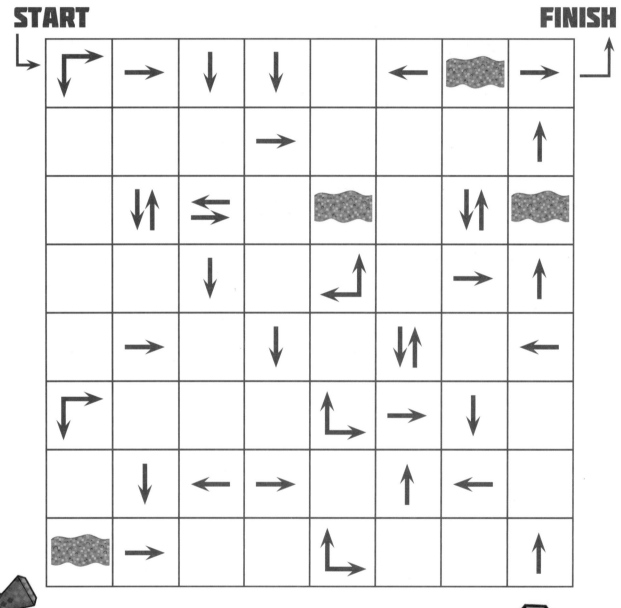

EPIC HUNT

Find and circle the names of 12 epic and rare drops in the word search. They might be forward, backward, up, down, or diagonal. Write unused letters on the blank spaces in order from top to bottom and left to right to discover something useful to know.

Hint: Circle individual letters instead of whole words to better isolate remaining letters. We've found one to get you started.

```
M  D  U  S  P  I  L  U  T  D  P  D
Y  P  U  I  R  O  O  D  N  O  R  I
G  R  S  M  A  R  G  E  W  E  P  P
I  C  E  D  F  R  R  E  O  P  U  V
K  S  F  T  A  O  R  R  O  M  C  I
P  C  I  N  A  E  T  G  T  A  R  N
Y  S  I  A  D  E  Y  E  X  O  E  E
P  T  P  R  A  B  P  L  K  E  T  S
E  S  A  T  B  A  P  E  A  C  T  W
A  I  S  R  A  B  N  O  R  I  U  Y
(L)(A)(V)(A)(B)(U)(C)(K)(E)(T) B  B
```

BRICK
BUCKET OF MUD
BUTTERCUP
GRANITE
IRON BARS
IRON DOOR
~~LAVA BUCKET~~
OXEYE DAISY
POWERED RAIL
REPEATER
TULIPS
VINES

___ ___ ___ ___ ___   ___ ___ ___   ___ ___   ___ ___ ___ ___

___ ___ ___ ___ ___   ___ ___ ___   ___ ___ ___

___ ___ ___ ___ ___ ___ ___ ___.   ___ ___ ___ ___   ___ ___ ___ ___ !

LOGIC IN THE MINE

Steve is trying to figure out where he found each block. Use his notes to help him figure out where each block was found.

Hint: Put an X in the box when you know that a block was not found in a place. Put an O in the box when you know where a block was found.

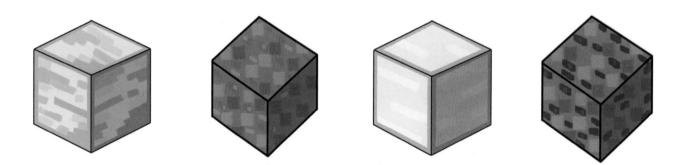

- Redstone was found in the cave.

- Diamond was found inside a building.

- Iron ore was not found in the woodland mansion or the ocean monument.

	Ravine	Woodland Mansion	Ocean Monument	Cave
IRON ORE				
REDSTONE				
GOLD				
DIAMOND				

FISHING LOGIC

Steve is trying to catch some fish.
Use the clues to help Steve find the fish.

Hint: *Put an X in the box when you know that a fish was not found in a place. Put an O in the box when you know where a fish was found.*

- Squid was under a plant.

- Blue fish was not in a plant.

- Pufferfish was locked in a box with gold.

- Shark was tangled in a plant.

	Under a Lily Pad	In a Sunken Ship	In a Sunken Treasure Chest	In the Kelp
BLUE FISH				
PUFFERFISH				
SQUID				
SHARK				

ZOMBIE RIDDLE

Use the picture-number combination to solve the riddle. The correct letter is the one where the picture and the number come together.

1	Y	P	E	L
2	O	K	R	A
3	H	M	T	D
4	S	B	W	I

Why won't the zombie eat turtle eggs with their hands?

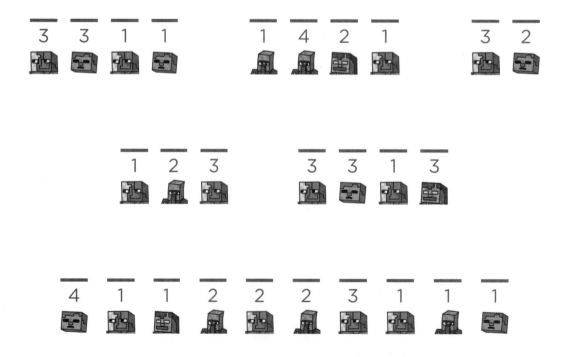

VILLAGERS RIDDLE

Use the picture-number combination to solve the riddle. The correct letter is the one where the picture and the number come together.

1	D	B	E	U
2	R	T	A	K
3	H	N	O	S
4	C	W	X	Y

Why do villagers hum?

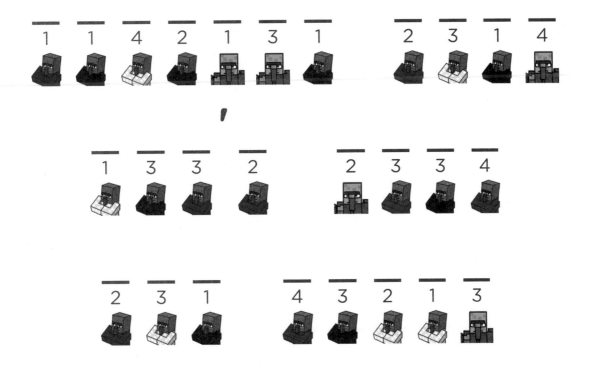

MINECRAFT SUDOKU 1

Draw the correct ocean mob in each square. The trick is to have only one of each mob in each 4 x 4 box, each column, and each row.

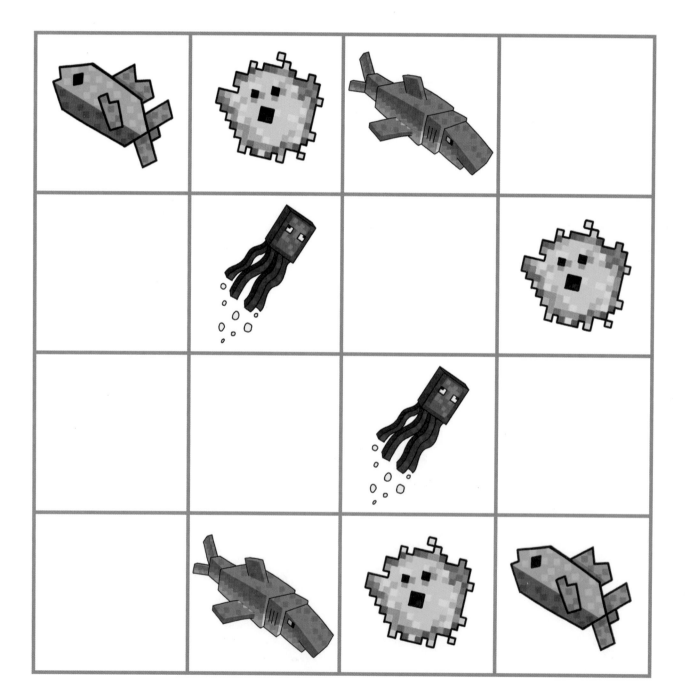

MINECRAFT SUDOKU 2

Draw the tool or weapon in each square. The trick is to have only one of each tool or weapon in each 4 x 4 box, each column, and each row.

MINECRAFT SUDOKU 3

Draw the mob from the farm in each square. The trick is to have only one of each mob in each 4 x 4 box, each column, and each row.

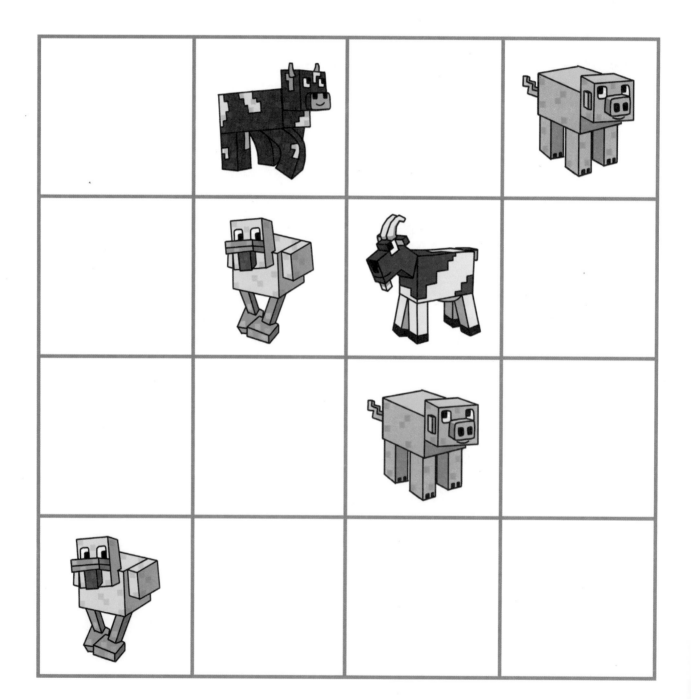

MINECRAFT SUDOKU 4

Draw a villager in each square. The trick is to have only one of each villager in each 4 x 4 box, each column, and each row.

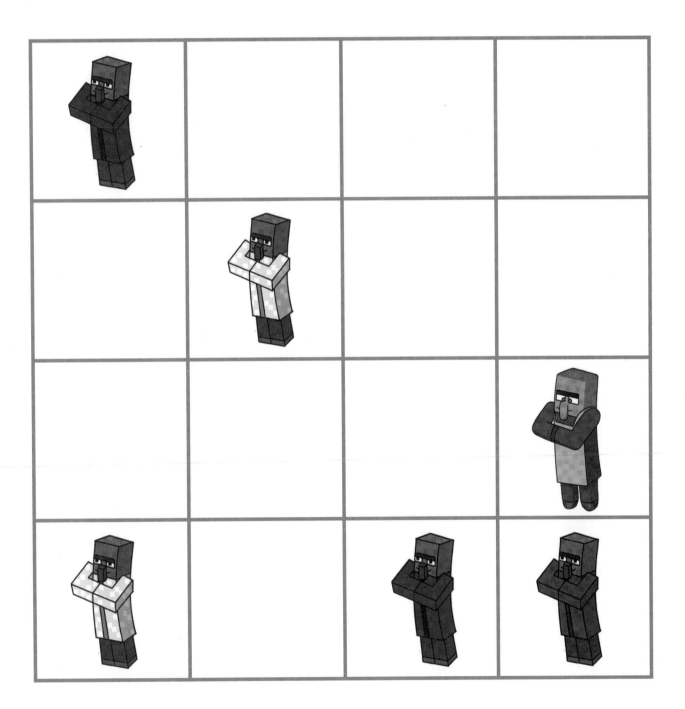

TARGET PRACTICE

Answer the questions to help skeleton practice shooting his arrows.

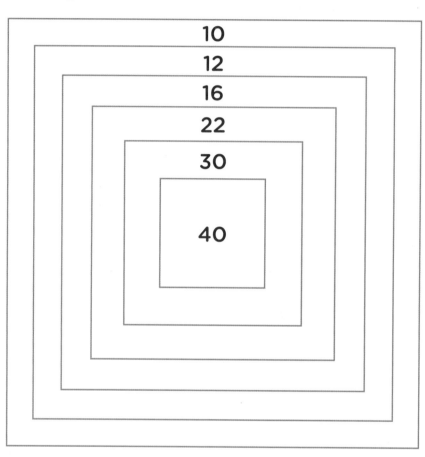

1. What is the highest score skeleton can get with 4 arrows, without hitting the same square more than once? _____

2. What is the lowest score skeleton can get with 4 arrows, without hitting the same number more than once? _____

3. How close to 100 can skeleton get without going over, using only 5 arrows? _____

4. No matter what numbers skeleton hits, the total is always an even number. Why? _____

BLOCK BUSTERS

Starting at the gold star, move from box to box, counting by twos. Write the letter from each box that you land on onto the lines below. If you place the letters in order, they will spell the answer to the riddle.

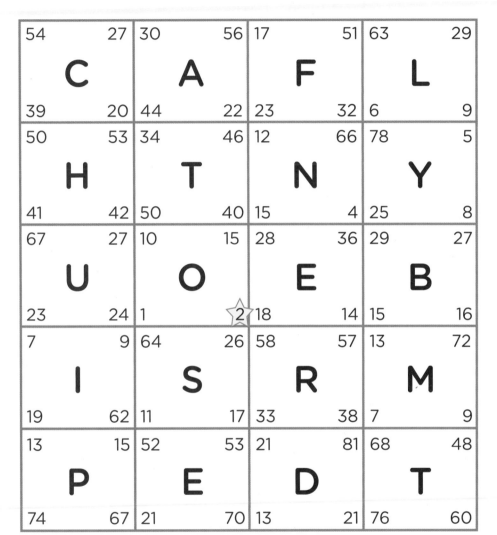

54 ... 27	30 ... 56	17 ... 51	63 ... 29
C	A	F	L
39 ... 20	44 ... 22	23 ... 32	6 ... 9
50 ... 53	34 ... 46	12 ... 66	78 ... 5
H	T	N	Y
41 ... 42	50 ... 40	15 ... 4	25 ... 8
67 ... 27	10 ... 15	28 ... 36	29 ... 27
U	O	E	B
23 ... 24	1 ... ☆2	18 ... 14	15 ... 16
7 ... 9	64 ... 26	58 ... 57	13 ... 72
I	S	R	M
19 ... 62	11 ... 17	33 ... 38	7 ... 9
13 ... 15	52 ... 53	21 ... 81	68 ... 48
P	E	D	T
74 ... 67	21 ... 70	13 ... 21	76 ... 60

How many blocks can Steve put in an empty cart?

__ __ __ __ __ __   __ __ __

__ __ __ __ __ __ __ __ __ __ __ __

__ __ __ __ __ __ __ __ __ __

,

__ __ __ __ ' __   __ __ __ __ __

SQUID WORDS

Follow the lines to unscramble words and phrases that describe squid.

1.

S	V	P	I	A	E	S

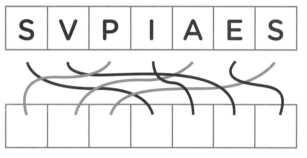

2.

S	A	R	E	G	H	I	M	T

3.

W	A	P	N	E	S	S	T	W	R	A	I	N

4.

K	O	N	D	R	S	A	S	P	I	S	C

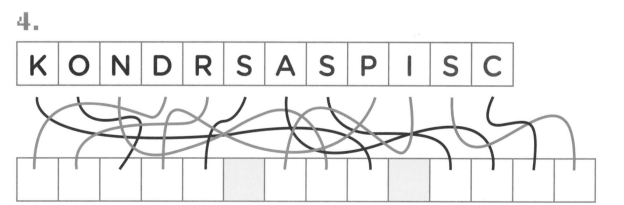

SPIDER WORDS

Follow the lines to unscramble words and phrases that describe spiders.

1.

T	U	N	R	L	E	A

2.

B	A	L	L	S	L	I	M	C	W	S

3.

N	O	N	L	A	W	S	P	E	V	A	E	S	S

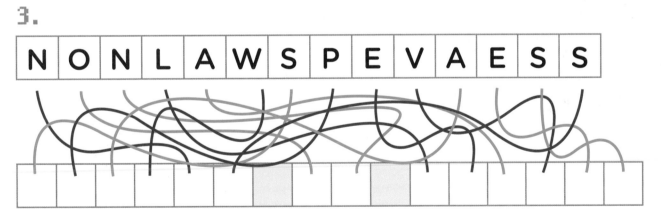

4.

S	A	D	R	T	I	O	P	N	G	S

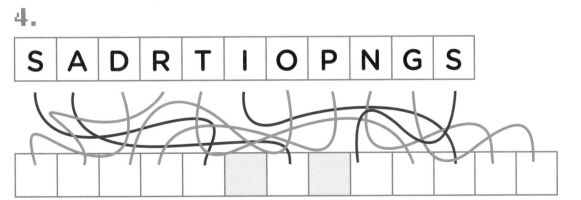

WHO'S WHERE?

Use the letter-box shapes as clues to find out who is where.

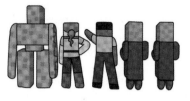

guardian	skeleton	wither	mooshroom
shulker	evoker	ghast	ocelot
librarian	dragon	witch	

1. The ⬜ w i ⬜ ⬜ e r is in the lava.

2. The ⬜⬜⬜⬜⬜⬜ flies over the entrance of the End.

3. The ⬜⬜⬜⬜⬜⬜⬜⬜ is by the ocean monument.

4. The ⬜⬜⬜⬜⬜⬜⬜⬜ wanders in the mushroom fields.

5. The 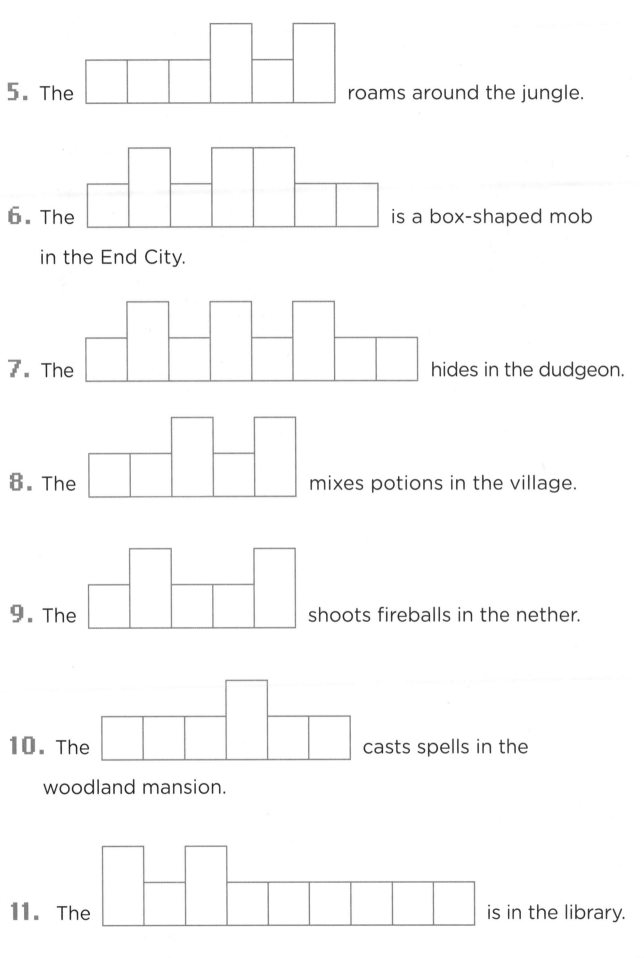 roams around the jungle.

6. The [   ] is a box-shaped mob in the End City.

7. The [   ] hides in the dudgeon.

8. The [   ] mixes potions in the village.

9. The [   ] shoots fireballs in the nether.

10. The [   ] casts spells in the woodland mansion.

11. The [   ] is in the library.

ANSWER KEY

PAGE 6
1. pig; 2. creeper; 3. horse; 4. spider

PAGE 10

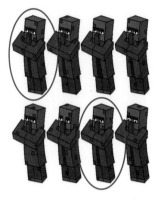

PAGE 16
1. C; 2. E; 3. A; 4. B; 5. D

PAGE 17
1. embarrassed; 2. sad; 3. happy; 4. proud;
5. angry; 6. bored

PAGE 22
NOBODY CAN TAKE AWAY MY POWER

PAGE 29
Boxes 1, 2, 4, 7, and 8 should be checked.

PAGE 38

START

FINISH

PAGE 39
If you can dream it, you can do it;
Goals will vary

PAGE 40
1. SURVIVE; 2. HOUSE; 3. TOOLS; 4. CREEPERS;
5. VILLAGERS

PAGE 42

		¹K				²B			
		I				R			
³C	O	N	F	I	D	E	N	⁴C	E
		D				A		A	
				⁵Y	E	T		L	
		⁶G			⁷H	⁸O	M	E	
		⁹G	R	I	T	N			
		O				E			
		W							
¹⁰S	E	T	A	G	O	A	L		
		H							

PAGES 70-71

TNT
5 gunpowder
+ 4 blocks of sand
———
9 items total

Bow
3 sticks
+ 3 pieces of string
———
6 items total

Arrows
1 stick
1 feather
+ 1 flint
———
3 items total

Enchantment Table
4 obsidian blocks
2 diamonds
+ 1 book
———
7 items total

Wood Pickaxe
2 sticks
+ 3 wood planks
———
5 items total

Bed
3 blocks of wool
+ 3 planks
———
6 items total

sticks
Arrow recipe

PAGES 88-89

1. What is Creeper's favorite color?

	4	4	2	21
	+5	+4	+3	+4
Answer	9	8	6	25
Letter	B	L	E	W

PAGES 88-89 (CONTINUED)

2. What is a witch's favorite subject in school?

	15	1	0	1	3	18	11	3
	+6	+3	+5	+7	+5	+8	+7	+17
Answer	21	4	5	8	8	26	18	20
Letter	S	P	E	L	L	I	N	G

PAGE 95

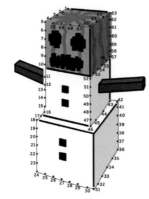

PAGE 96
4, 8, 13, 17, 21, 24, 25, 30, 32, 36, 44, 47, 49, 53, 56, 58, 60, 61, 64, 67, 70, 73, 75, 76, 78, 81, 82, 85, 89, 94, 97

PAGE 97
CREEPER; ZOMBIE PIGMAN

PAGE 98
2, 4, 6, 8, 10, 12, 14, 16

PAGE 99
1. 3; 2. 6; 3. 9; 4. 12; 5. 15; 6. 18; 7. 21

PAGE 100
5, 10, 15, 20, 25, 30, 35, 40, 45, 50, 55, 60, 65, 70, 75, 80, 85, 90, 95, 100, 105

PAGE 101
10, 20, 30, 40, 50, 60, 70, 80, 90

PAGE 102

PAGE 103

PAGE 104
1. =; 2. >; 3. <; 4. =; 5. <; 6. >; 7. >; 8. <; 9. =; 10. <; 11. <; 12. <

PAGE 105
1. 9 eggs; 2. 6 carrots; 3. 7 pigs; 4. 8 sheep

PAGE 106
1. 2; 2. 1; 3. 4; 4. 5; 5. 7; 6; 7. 3; 8. 8

He had a blast!

PAGE 107
1. 5; 2. 4; 3. 3; 4. 3

PAGE 108

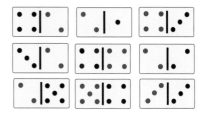

PAGE 109
1. 4; 2. 2; 3. 4; 4. 3; 5. 2; 6. 2; 7. 2; 8. 3; 9. 7

PAGE 110
1. 8; 2. 5; 3. 7; 4. 6; 5. 3; 6. 4

PAGE 111
1. 2 blue, 8 red; 2. 9 blue, 1 red; 3. 7 blue, 3 red; 4. 10 blue, 0 red; 5. 8 blue, 2 red; 6. 6 blue, 4 red

PAGE 112
1. 13; 2. 17; 3. 18; 4. 14; 5. 12; 6. 15

PAGE 113

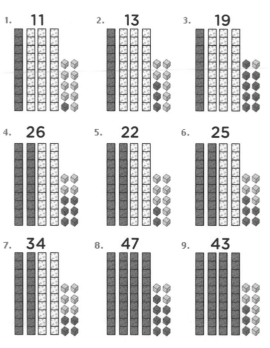

PAGE 114

1. 52	2. 37	3. 24
Tens | Ones	Tens | Ones	Tens | Ones
5 | 2	3 | 7	2 | 4

4. 16	5. 20	6. 41
Tens | Ones	Tens | Ones	Tens | Ones
1 | 6	2 | 0	4 | 1

7. 52	8. 93	9. 75
Tens | Ones	Tens | Ones	Tens | Ones
5 | 2	9 | 3	7 | 5

PAGE 115

1. 82	2. 56	3. 70
Tens | Ones	Tens | Ones	Tens | Ones
8 | 2	5 | 6	7 | 0

4. 61	5. 12	6. 79
Tens | Ones	Tens | Ones	Tens | Ones
6 | 1	1 | 2	7 | 9

7. 95	8. 26	9. 33
Tens | Ones	Tens | Ones	Tens | Ones
9 | 5	2 | 6	3 | 3

PAGE 116

1. 3 + 4 = 7; 4 + 3 = 7; 7 − 3 = 4; 7 − 4 = 3
2. 5 + 1 = 6; 1 + 5 = 6; 6 − 1 = 5; 6 − 5 = 1
3. 2 + 6 = 8; 2 + 6 = 8; 8 − 2 = 6; 8 − 6 = 2
4. 7 + 2 = 9; 2 + 7 = 9; 9 − 7 = 2; 9 − 2 = 7

PAGE 117

1. 8 + 3 = 11; 11 − 3 = 8; 11 − 8 = 3
2. 5 + 4 = 9; 9 − 4 = 5; 9 − 5 = 4
3. 7 + 6 = 13; 13 − 6 = 7; 13 − 7 = 6
4. 4 + 8 = 12; 12 − 8 = 4; 12 − 4 = 8

PAGE 118

1. 30; 2. 60; 3. 40; 4. 54; 5. 72; 6. 81; 7. 25; 8. 46

PAGE 119

1. 20; 2. 50; 3. 40; 4. 33; 5. 62; 6. 6; 7. 17; 8. 71

PAGE 121

Shape	How Many Sides?	How Many Corners?
triangle	3	3
rhombus	4	4
rectangle	4	4
circle	0	0
square	4	4
hexagon	6	6

PAGE 122

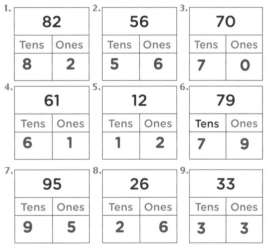

PAGE 124

1. 10:00; 2. 3:00; 3. 7:00; 4. 2:30; 5. 8:30; 6. 6:30

PAGE 125

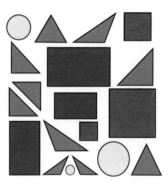

PAGE 126

1. $\frac{1}{4}$ 2. $\frac{1}{2}$ 3. $\frac{4}{6}$ 4. $\frac{2}{3}$ 5. $\frac{5}{8}$

6. $\frac{1}{3}$ 7. $\frac{2}{5}$ 8. $\frac{4}{7}$ 9. $\frac{2}{4}$ 10. $\frac{4}{8}$

PAGE 127

Answers will vary.

PAGE 128

1. 12 cm; 2. 16 cm; 3. 16 cm; 4. 18 cm; 5. 18 cm;
6. 20 cm; 7. 20 cm; 8. 16 cm; 9. 16 cm

PAGE 129

1. 18 cm; 2. 18 cm; 3. 25 cm; 4. 20 cm; 5. 64 cm;
6. 28 cm; 7. 10 cm; 8. 24 cm

PAGE 130

1. 1, 2 or 12; 2. 4, 3 or 43; 3. 6, 7 or 67;
4. 5, 0 or 50; 5. 2, 2 or 22; 6. 8, 1 or 81;
7. 9, 8 or 98; 8. 7, 4, or 74

PAGE 131

1. 6, 1, 8; 61, 8; 618
2. 3, 4, 7; 34, 7; 347
3. 5, 2, 3; 52, 3; 523
4. 6, 0, 7; 60, 7; 607
5. 1, 8, 5; 18, 5; 185

PAGE 132

1. 3,579; 2. 4,091; 3. 3,000; 4. 7,778; 5. 6,003;
6. 1,364; 7. 5,891; 8. 8,001

PAGE 133

1. 500; 2. 5; 3. 7,000, 2; 4. 100, 10;
5. 9,000, 20, 6; 6. 200, 50; 7. 4,000, 600, 2;
8. 6,000, 200, 10, 9

PAGE 134

1. 35; 2. 57; 3. 67; 4. 67; 5. 68; 6. 77

PAGE 135

1. 28; 2. 77; 3. 76; 4. 57; 5. 88; 6. 94; 7. 74; 8. 67;
9. 73; RED DIAMONDS

PAGE 136

1. 22; 2. 24; 3. 23; 4. 24; 5. 31; 6. 37

PAGE 137

1. 52; 2. 30; 3. 21; 4. 42; 5. 31; 6. 25; 7. 30; 8. 24;
9. 21; A MUSHROOM

PAGE 138

1. 32; 2. 77; 3. 78; 4. 37; 5. 26; 6. 78; A FENCE

PAGE 139

1. 38; 2. 7; 3. 16; 4. 21; answers will vary

PAGE 140

60

PAGE 141

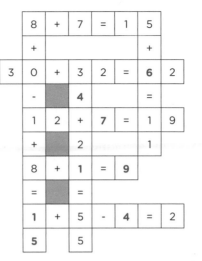

8	+	7	=	1	5		
+					+		
3	0	+	3	2	=	6	2
-		4			=		
1	2	+	7	=	1	9	
+		2			1		
8	+	1	=	9			
=		=					
1	+	5	-	4	=	2	
5		5					

PAGE 142

2. 2, 11; 3. 7, 2, 25; 4. 9, 13, 28; 5. 12, 9, 29; 6. 17,
13; 7. 9, 1, 6; 8. 14, 16; 9. 9, 15, 24

PAGE 143

2. 5, 2, 15; 3. 2, 10, 10, 16; 4. 17, 12, 17, 29;
5. 3, 5, 11, 28, 52; 6. Answers will vary.

PAGE 144

1. 3 + 3 + 3 = 9, 3 + 2 + 2 = 7, 5 – 2 = 3, 3, 2, 5
2. 6 + 6 = 12, 10 – 6 = 4, 10 + 4 = 14, 6, 10, 4
3. 4 + 4 + 4 = 12, 4 + 8 + 8 = 20, 8 – 2 = 6, 4, 8, 2
4. 8 + 8 = 16, 10 + 10 + 8 = 28, 10 + 8 + 4 = 22, 8, 10, 4

PAGE 146

1. C; 2. A; 3. B; 4. E; 5. D

PAGE 147

1. short; 2. long; 3. short; 4. short; 5. short;
6. long; 7. short; 8. short; 9. long

PAGE 148

1. E; 2. C; 3. B; 4. A; 5. D

PAGE 149

1. map; 2. egg; 3. fish; 4. block; 5. web; 6. bat;
7. hug; 8. squid

PAGE 150

1. cake; 2. bone; 3. mule; 4. ride; 5. cube

PAGE 151

1. C; 2. A; 3. E; 4. D; 5. B

PAGE 152

1. bread (short); 2. dream (long); 3. peak (long);
4. head (short); 5. meat (long)

PAGE 153
1. Beach (long); 2. seat (long); 3. team (long);
4. beat (long); 5. dead (short)

PAGE 154
1. farm; 2. furry; 3. dirt; 4. horse; 5. bark; 6. flower

PAGE 155
1. cart; 2. park; 3. art; 4. hard; 5. dark

PAGE 156
1. flight; 2. right; 3. sight; 4. might; 5. bright

PAGE 157
1. night; 2. sight; 3. bright; 4. fight; 5. flight

PAGE 158

```
P Y D O B T S A F J
M L T T P D S O T T
U D F B A M O A N D
J D A E T D A E L Z
R M R M T S W C M B
T L C E T B I I J T
L P S M S M U Z N L
B T I L E A D I E D
D N D L H T N R L N
D P W Q C V L D V D
```

PAGE 159

```
T R I D E R K E B W
R E Y H E L C R N X
A Y K W O A T D A N
C D O A L R K T D B
B L M P T R S R I X
F U R R Y D O E A L
K D R A H A M N N P
N T M Y N R B E L X
O R R W A K W M T Y
W A J F N X N B T K
```

PAGE 160
1. blast; 2. sand; 3. fast; 4. chest; 5. craft

PAGE 161
1. jump; 2. test; 3. camp; 4. mind; 5. wind

PAGE 162
1. block; 2. clock; 3. torch; 4. bush; 5. church

PAGE 163
1. much; 2. rich; 3. wish; 4. search; 5. rush

PAGE 164
1. Bring; 2. ring; 3. wing; 4. string; 5. sting

PAGE 165
1. sing; 2. king; 3. sling; 4. cling; 5. spring

PAGE 166
1. D; 2. A; 3. E; 4. C; 5. B

PAGE 167
1. chest; 2. shears; 3. shield; 4. thread; 5. wheat;
6. house; 7. torch; 8. Bed

PAGES 168–169
Answers may vary.

PAGE 170
1. mean; 2. people who live in a place; 3. to create;
4. places

PAGE 171
1. neither bad nor good; 2. a swampy forest;
3. nothing there; 4. dangerous

PAGE 172
1. D; 2. C; 3. A; 4. B

PAGE 173
1. gives; 2. open; 3. Inside; 4. up

PAGE 174
1. on; 2. in; 3. in front of; 4. beside, behind

PAGE 175
1. by; 2. on; 3. in; 4. above; 5. beside

PAGES 176–177
1. W - It is the center of everything. 2. W - It
is made of clay and glass. 3. W / P - It has tall
buildings. 4. W - Inhabitants and visitors.
5. W / P – You can walk, ride the train, or take a
boat.

PAGES 178–179
1. shark, squid, or crab; 2. two; 3. purple;
4. the shark; 5. the squid

PAGE 182
4, 3, 1, 2

PAGE 183
2, 1, 4, 3

PAGE 184

PAGE 185
1. pigs; 2. potatoes; 3. witches' 4. cows; 5. bushes

PAGE 186
1. fight; 2. swim; 3. eat; 4. laugh; 5. run; 6. ride;
7. fly; 8. think; 9. sit

PAGE 187
1. D; 2. B; 3. E; 4. A; 5. C

PAGE 188
Adjective choices may vary. Possibilities:
1. red <u>barn</u>; 2. noisy <u>cow</u>; 3. spotted <u>cat</u>;
4. hungry <u>horse</u>; 5. beautiful <u>butterfly</u>;
6. furry <u>cat</u>; 7. white <u>rabbit</u>

PAGE 189
1. <u>oinked</u> loudly; 2. <u>walked</u> aimlessly; 3. <u>petted</u>
gently; 4. <u>hopped</u> quickly; 5. <u>sat</u> sleepily;
6. <u>floated</u> slowly; 7. <u>waited</u> patiently

PAGE 192
1. bee, be; 2. acts, axe; 3. I, eye; 4. flour, flower;
5. which, witch

PAGE 193
Answers will vary.

PAGE 194
1. zombies, player 2. The zombies attacked the
player. 3. The sun peered through the window
and the zombies were gone.

PAGE 195
1. villager, witch, player 2. A witch appeared
when the villager was struck by lightning.
3. The witch ran away.

PAGE 196
1. C; 2. C; 3. B

PAGE 197
1. B; 2. A; 3. Answers will vary.

PAGE 198
Answers will vary.

PAGE 199
No, because Steve did not see the chicken today.

PAGE 200
1. Villager; 2. Alex; 3. Steve; 4. Skeleton

PAGE 201
Answers will vary.

PAGE 204
1. to the library; 2. to find a book of
enchantment to defeat the wither. 3. Yes

PAGE 208
Answers will vary but may include:

How to Build a Snowman
- roll the snow into balls
- add a carrot nose
- add coal for eyes

(shared) need snow

How to Build a Snow Golem
- need a shovel
- need a crafting table
- need a pumpkin head
- punch the snow with the shovel

PAGE 209
Answers will vary.

PAGES 210–211
1. sandstone; 2. hot; 3. temple; 4. a chest;
5. valuable loot; 6. answers will vary but may
include "something of great worth";
7. husks; 8. rotten flesh

PAGE 212

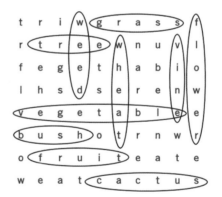

PAGE 213

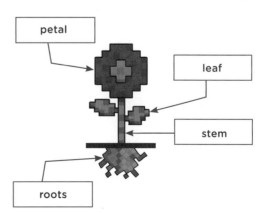

petal

leaf

stem

roots

PAGE 214

PAGE 215

Wait.
5

Drop a seed in the hole.
2

Cover the seed with dirt.
3

Make a hole in the dirt.
1

Soon you will have a plant.
6

Water the ground.
4

PAGE 216
1. food; 2. Sunlight; 3. air; 4. shelter; 5. water

PAGE 217
1. Thursday, Friday, Sunday
2. Tuesday, Wednesday
3. Answer will vary.
4. Answer will vary.

PAGE 218

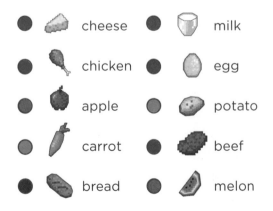

cheese   milk

chicken   egg

apple   potato

carrot   beef

bread   melon

PAGE 219

1 B	2 A	N	A	3 N	A		4 E	G	5 G
	P			U		6 M			R
	7 P	R	O	T	E	I	N		A
	L			S		L			I
8 M	E	A	T			K			N
									S

PAGE 221
1. hands; 2. mouth; 3. teeth; 4. bath;
5. food; 6. sleep

PAGE 222
1. see; 2. smell; 3. taste; 4. hear; 5. touch

PAGE 224
1. Evoker; 2. casts spells; 3. Creeper;
4. exploded; 5. Iron golem; 6. gave the villager
a flower; 7. Blaze; 8. a hostile mob

PAGE 225
Answers will vary.

PAGE 226
1. The snow golem is a mob. 2. It has two
snow blocks and a pumpkin head. 3. It throws
snowballs. 4. Does it melt when it gets hot?
5. Does it melt in the rain?

PAGE 227
1. !
2. .
3. ?
4. ?
5. .
6. .
7. !
8. .

PAGE 228
1. Steve cuts the cake. 2. Dragon flies through
blocks. 3. Trees grow in the Overworld. 4. Alex
cares for chickens and pigs.

PAGE 229
Answers will vary.

PAGE 230
1. Alex, Minecraft; 2. Steve, Mindcraft Mining;
3. In, April; 4. On, Monday, Creeper;
5. Ender, Dragon, End

PAGE 231

The Desert Biome is made up of sandstone. It is very dry and hot. Very few plants and animals live in the desert. Golden rabbits can live there. Cacti can live there, too. In some deserts, there may be a desert temple. It is usually buried in the ground. Desert temples are dark. In the center of the temple, there is a desert chest. It is filled with valuable loot. At night, husks will spawn in the desert. Many players avoid the desert, but not Steve. He likes to visit the desert in June when it is really hot. Sometimes Alex will go with him. They have fun. Sometimes they look for the desert chest.

PAGES 232–233

1. Clouds float in the sky.
2. The creeper wears a cowboy hat.
3. The Enderman wins the race.
4. The horse eats a carrot.
5. Watch out for the lava.
6. Puffer fish are poisonous.
7. Mushrooms grow in the Nether.
8. Creepers do not have teeth.
9. This sheep is dyed pink.
10. Skeletons are hostile mobs.

PAGES 234–237
Answers will vary.

PAGE 238
1. shoots; 2. crawls; 3. crafts; 4. falls

PAGE 239
1. rides; 2. laugh; 3. sleep; 4. hops

PAGE 240
1. runs; 2. play; 3. fights; 4. rides

PAGE 241
1. The skeletons <u>march</u> in groups of four.
2. The shulker <u>hides</u> in its shell.
3. Nitwit <u>reads</u> a map. 4. Alex <u>fights</u> the ghast.

PAGE 242
1. is; 2. are; 3. has; 4. have

PAGE 243
1. is; 2. are; 3. has; 4. have; 5. am

PAGE 244
1. was; 2. is; 3. am; 4. was; 5. were

PAGE 245
Answers will vary.

PAGE 246
1. Ghast is the meanest mob. 2. Shulkers are silly mobs. 3. Zombie piglins are the most dangerous mobs. 4. The evoker is very sneaky.

PAGE 247
Answers will vary.

PAGE 248
Answers will vary.

PAGE 254
1. didn't; 2. couldn't; 3. wasn't; 4. can't; 5. Don't

PAGE 255

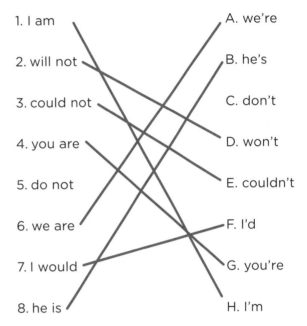

1. I am
2. will not
3. could not
4. you are
5. do not
6. we are
7. I would
8. he is

A. we're
B. he's
C. don't
D. won't
E. couldn't
F. I'd
G. you're
H. I'm

PAGE 256

Nouns	Verbs	Adjectives
pumpkin	hide	scary
mob	attack	golden
biome	dig	hostile
villager	laugh	funny
bird	climb	green

PAGE 257
Answers will vary but might include the details below.
1. The bright red mushroom has white spots and a short brown stem.
2. The coiled snake is baring its fangs and looks ready to strike.
3. Steve is sleeping peacefully in his bed.
4. The zombie is fleeing the hot lava pit before it swallows him up.

PAGE 279

Answers will vary but might include:
1. Alex is wearing a different shirt; 2. Alex is patting a different animal; 3. The chicken's wing is rounded in one picture and square in the other; 4. Alex's ponytail is larger in one picture; 5. Alex is wearing a belt in one picture; 6. Alex's hand is rounded in one picture and square in the other; 7. The chicken is looking straight ahead in one picture and to the side in the other picture; 8. Alex's feet are larger and darker in one picture.

PAGE 280

THEY ARE AFRAID OF FLYING OFF THE HANDLE!

PAGE 281

Wither: we, he, hi, it, hit, the, wet, tie, her, whit, wire, tier, tire, threw, white, write, their

Witch: hi, it, hit, itch, with, wit, whit, tic

PAGE 282

IT WAS FEELING ROTTEN.

PAGE 283

Iron golem: no, on, go, in, gem, men, gel, leg, log, moo, rim, ego, rig, ion, lie, grin, girl, more, ring, room, lime, limo, long, glim, germ, mine, mole, mile, loner, liner, reign, rein, miler, miner, minor, lingo, melon, groom, gloom, region, looming, gloomier

Snow golem: on, me, ow, we, no, so, mow, sow, ego, new, low, men, gem, sew, moo, own, owl, one, slow, owns, owls, mole, moon, lows, long, gems, glow, gown, meow, goose, moose, swoon, moons, moles, women, lemon, loosen

PAGE 284

bow, cow, how, hot, hat, bat

PAGE 285

Creeper and Enderman

PAGE 286

ghast, ghost, host, lost, last, fast, fat, cat

PAGE 287

cobblestone and grass

PAGE 288

HE NEEDED A PUMPKIN PATCH.

PAGE 289

Diamond: do, am, ad, an, in, on, aim, mad, man, nod, and, dad, odd, mind, maid, amino, domain, dam, dim, din, don, did, main, add, id, aid, amid

Emerald: am, ad, arm, eel, ear, are, red, rad, mad, dare, read, real, deal, medal, armed, elder, dream, leader, era, ream, mere, mare, meld, male, meal, made, mead, ale, ade, lad, lead, led, lame, alder, elm, marl, realm, deem, deer, dear, reel, dam, dame

PAGE 290

HE WANTED TO FIND 14 CARROTS GOLD.

PAGE 291

Librarian: an, in, bin, lab, bar, rib, ran, air, bail, barn, nail, rain, liar, brain, lair, bin, ban, bran, rail, nib, nab, nil

Enderman: am, an, me, mad, man, men, end, rad, ran, ear, are, made, mean, name, dean, need, dare, dear, deer, near, read, named, armed, earned, neared, renamed, and, era, mead, mere, mend, demean, mare, mane, nerd, ream, ram, red, darn, dream, reed, rend

PAGE 292

PAGE 293

Wooly Cow - Trishenanigan
Cluckshroom - CL Loves Green
Jumbo Rabbit - Steffeefee
Jolly Llama - Jana Banana

PAGE 294

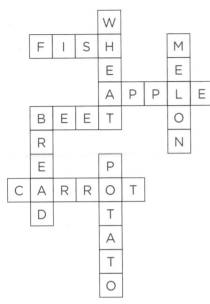

THE STEAMED CARROT; THE ESTEEMED CARROT

PAGE 295

PAGE 296

START

PAGE 297

NO PROB-LLAMA!

PAGE 298

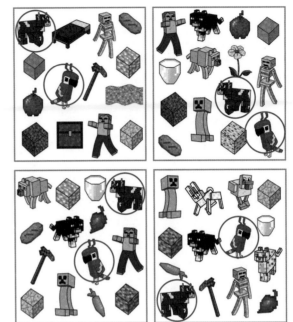

PAGE 299

Min and Phillipe reach the ore to mine diamonds.

PAGE 300

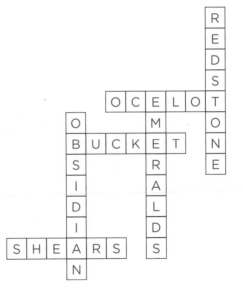

A CLUCKSHROOM (A cluck shhhh room. Get it?)

PAGE 301

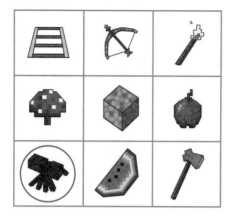

PAGE 302

PAGE 303

OVER-KOALA-FIED (Yeah, that's a joke.)

PAGE 304

PAGE 305

Only M-Earth Gal gets to claim the Jolly Llama.

PAGE 306

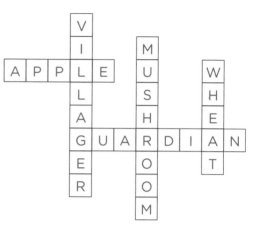

A PERSISTENT HOLOGRAM

PAGE 307

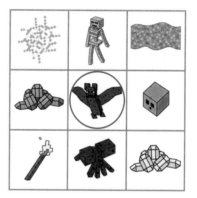

PAGE 308

PAGE 309
MOB OF ME; Of course you're the most special mob in Minecraft Earth!

PAGE 310
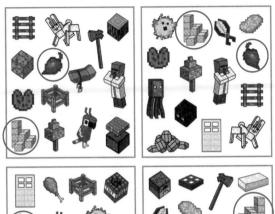

PAGE 311
Mindy, Mia, and Milton join Matthew for the Adventure. Max does not.

PAGE 312

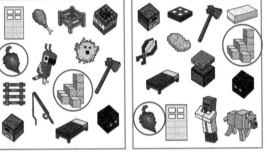

CLAW ENFORCEMENT

PAGE 313
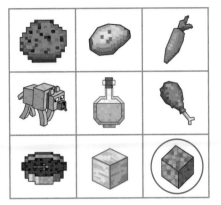

PAGE 314

START   FINISH

PAGE 315
HILL-ARIOUS

PAGE 316

353

PAGE 317

Ella is the only player to reach the life-sized moobloom statue.

PAGE 318

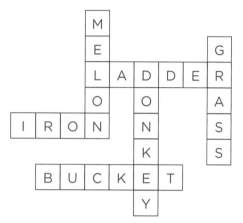

AUGMENTED REALITY

PAGE 319

PAGE 320

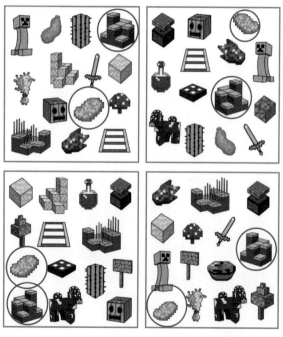

PAGE 321

Ben - Diamonds
Jake - Rubies
Bella - Emeralds
Jayda - Iron ore

PAGE 322

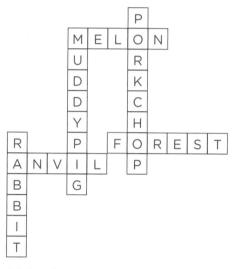

FOOD CANNOT BE COOKED
DURING AN ADVENTURE

PAGE 323

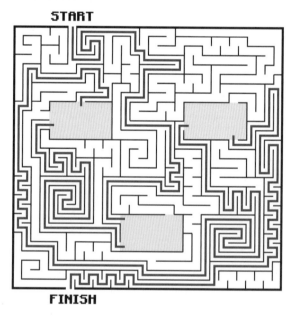

PAGE 324

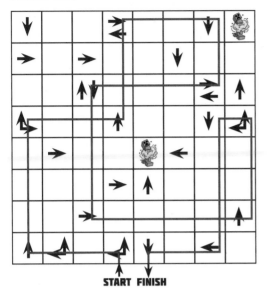

PAGE 325

D	G	I	P	Y	M	M	U	G	P
U	Y	G	D	D	U	M	M	U	M
M	M	I	M	M	D	U	D	M	M
M	U	P	M	D	Y	D	I	U	v
Y	D	Y	Y	P	I	G	D	D	I
P	P	D	D	N	M	Y	Y	D	Y
I	M	D	G	P	P	P	D	Y	D
G	M	U	D	I	I	I	D	G	D
M	U	M	G	P	G	G	U	I	U
G	U	P	Y	D	D	U	M	P	M

PAGE 326

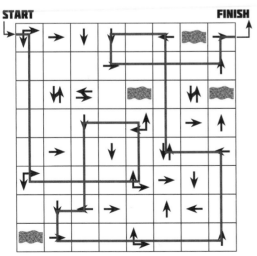

PAGE 327

Muddy pigs are epic drops from pig tappables. Tap away!

PAGE 328

iron ore, ravine; redstone, cave; gold, ocean monument; diamond, woodland mansion

PAGE 329

blue fish, in a sunken ship; pufferfish, in a sunken treasure chest; squid, under a lily pad; shark, in the kelp

PAGE 330

THEY LIKE TO EAT THEM SEPARATELY.

PAGE 331

BECAUSE THEY DON'T KNOW THE WORDS.

PAGE 332

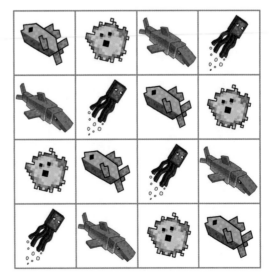

PAGE 333

PAGE 334

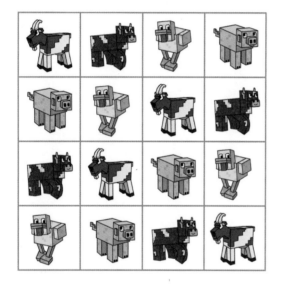

PAGE 335

PAGE 336

1. 108; 2. 60; 3. 90
4. Because they are all even numbers.

PAGE 337

ONLY ONE BECAUSE AFTER THAT THE CART ISN'T EMPTY.

PAGE 338

1. passive; 2. eight arms; 3. spawns in water;
4. drops ink sacs

PAGE 339

1. neutral; 2. climbs walls; 3. spawns on leaves;
4. drops a sting

PAGES 340-341

1. wither; 2. dragon; 3. guardian; 4. mooshroom;
5. ocelot; 6. shulker; 7. skeleton; 8. witch;
9. ghast; 10. evoker; 11. librarian